SHE WASN'T LOST

SHE WASN'T LOST

By: Rochelle Robertson

CONTENTS

Dedication

This book is dedicated to Denise Green-Williams,

Gwendolyn Hollies and Roger Hollies. May your souls rest

in eternal peace.

Preface

Being an adopted child was never easy. Well at least not for Sarah, it seems like she was lost and could not be found. Sarah always felt confused and lost, as if she would wander helplessly within her own mind. She was drifting down extremely gloomy roads alone. Sarah often noticed how she could disappear in all of her life's turmoil. She would get stuck in that dark pit of trouble and despair, feeling handcuffed and chained to the tortuous thoughts that confined her.

The mere idea of adoption always evoked feelings of neglect and abandonment. Her own parents turning her over to the bondages of worthlessness and uselessness. Sarah never felt good enough. Deep down in her heart, Sarah felt like she was never good enough for her parents to get their act together, what could it have taken for them to sacrifice care a bit more about their children? She thought to herself late at night, "How are my parents sleeping at night, knowing their children are in the care of a complete stranger?"

She wondered if they ever had a peace of mind. Sarah questioned everything that took place leading up to the main event which landed her and her sibling in foster care. "Why are my parents leaving me to the system?" "Do they not love me or my brother?" "Why were they so selfish?" She honestly dreaded the answer but longed to know what they would respond to her questions

Sarah suffered. She believed answers were owed to her from her parents, not from other family members. She believed they deserved to know, she deserved that much. Unfortunately, she would never know their answers because her mother is sick with a mental disease known as schizophrenia and her dad is dead.

Schizophrenia is a disorder that affects an individual's ability to think, feel and behave properly. The disease causes hallucination, hallucination, paranoia, hearing voices, depressions, fear, and delusion.

Though Sarah's mom suffered with schizophrenia all of her life, her father could have picked up the slack. Instead he backpedaled from his responsibilities at the early age of two. These tragic happenings placed Sarah in a position of future encounters of self-absorption, trauma, and torment.

Sarah is one of the 6 children her mother gave birth to. There are 4 girls and two boys, all of whom have suffered in some way, because of their mother's unwanted and helpless affliction, mental disease.

Introduction

It all started about 24 years ago, Sarah and her brother Patrick were the two of the four children that were swept away to foster care. The chain of events and mangled story has yet to unwound in a liberating truth. Many stories have been told by different family members, those that were present at the time it all went down. However, Sarah frankly never knew, and still doesn't know what story to rely on.

The time of wondering has about come to an end. The damage done has already brought turmoil into Sarah's existence. Yet, through all of the bad deliveries she has not stopped loving her parents. Sarah's love for her parents grew over the years and is still growing. All she ever wanted was certainty. She thought she needed a legitimate reason for her parents allowing such a wrenching pain to take their place, but she soon realized that the only closure she would receive would be from God's unending love for her. Sarah tried accepting the possibility she didn't and would never have all the answers to those mind-boggling questions. All of what she was searching for was far from her spiritual understanding. God had to reveal Himself to her so that she could know that loneliness was really deception.

Spiritually we should seek GOD, our Lord, and Savior for all of our understanding. We must cast our burdens on Him.

Sarah thought there was a time she found God or maybe He noticed her. However, as life progressed, she lost sight of GOD place in her life. Though Sarah days in foster care were very short lived. She remembered some events with clarity as if they happened yesterday. She was roughly two years old, and her brother Patrick was 4 years old at the time of being placed.

Sarah would often reminisce during her stay with her foster mother. She would recall the church visits, nighttime prayers, presents, tantalizing breakfasts, and super delicious suppers. There were twin foster sisters who lived with them as well. Sarah made sure to always acknowledge the woman who, in her phenomenon, self-sacrificing, and open heart, took in children who involuntarily landed on her doorstep. Most days Sarah was wholeheartedly grateful and thankful for her foster mother. Even in her teen years and adult years, despite situations that sometimes cause conflict, her foster mom held a special place in her heart. Their time was limited together but the bond remained.

Shortly after being in foster care, sometime between 6 months to a year; Sarah's older sister Shanice and her then-husband James went to court to battle for them. They wanted the guardian rights of both Sarah and her brother Patrick. Considering Sarah's mother wasn't well and her dad having relinquished his rights, it was best that they be cared for a sibling. For Sarah, it was bittersweet being an adopted child. Her name is Sarah, this is her story, and I am going to tell it the best way I know how.

Chapter 1

At age fifteen, Sarah began suffering from a subconscious mental condition known as, Abandoned Child Syndrome. This condition results primarily from the loss of one or both parents or sexual abuse. Abandonment may be physical (the parents are not present in the child's life) or emotional (resulting in the parents withholding affection, nurturing or stimulation). Sarah would have never fathom the sufferings she would bring into the lives of her adopting siblings.

Shanice and her husband James took on the responsibility of Sarah and Patrick. They inherited them physically and mentally. Sarah, in her sister's care, started battling the psychological condition that impaired good behavior. The ravage done to Sarah, not having her biological parents in her life, had begun to ruined her. The wounds forming in Sarah's life, developed over the years, were undetected, and the pain struck deep in her heart and mind.

Sarah's painful wounds seeped with sorrow. Her pain became significantly unfathomable and for years, it rode piggy back. Healing didn't come, instead it became her bitter truth.

Oftentimes, we may be unaware of the amount of hurt a friend or family member is experiencing. We may or may not notice a change in behavior, see emotional injury, and we can misunderstand what it is they really need from us. Some of us may not know how to help our love ones, so we ignore what seems to be a hopeless situation. We sometimes try to help the loved one but things don't always take the turns we planned. We must learn to recognize emotional injuries, understand and accept the process, or else we hinder victim's healing. The pain could linger on within them, thereby, destroying their childhood and even adult life.

Maybe Patrick was stronger than she was. Sarah believed being adopted, never affected her brother Patrick. She never asked Patrick personally how he conquered his emotions of having their parents stripped from his life. It just became a taboo subject Sarah and Patrick never spoke of to one another. Even though she saw her brother every day, her thoughts ran rampart. She battled with her feelings and what seemed to be his lack thereof, all of this happening during her endless mental trials and tribulations.

Occasionally, we go through things alongside our loved ones whether it be aunt, dad, brother, sister or friend. We expect them to hold our hands for as long as we think we need them to. When they release our hand before we are ready, over time, those feelings of abandonment can begin to surface.

Sarah never told Patrick to stay a little while longer. She never expressed that she had some security in knowing he was there. She wanted him to stick around until she could, independently, confront the mental soldiers that waged war against her. She just expected Patrick to know she needed him and did not want to go through life without him. She thought they would be two peas in a pod, taking on the world together. That planned fail through, like many others, it just did not go the way she thought it would.

Time passed and Sarah could see Patrick easily carrying on with his life. Patrick went on to get good jobs and nice cars, he eventually started a family of his own. Patrick became successful and independent. It was bittersweet for her. She wanted him and her other siblings to thrive, flourish, and conquer any demon they had. Unfortunately, Sarah was left alone to fight her demons. She was waging war alone, in the war of mental turmoil. Standing alone, she watched him accomplish his goals, while she struggled to dig trenches where she could hide during the battle.

Sarah was raised with Shanice and her husband James's kids, Sarah nieces and nephews. Growing up beside them was a challenge. She became very envious of her nieces and nephews. Sarah saw the support and the bond they had with their parents. She oftentimes felt the hurt of motherless love and would burry herself deep within her thoughts. Sarah longed for that same love, support, and affection. Deep down she knew she may never be able to receive attention and affection from her parents, and instead would have to receive what she could from sister and brother-in-law.

Resentment took root in her heart and anger grew. In the horrible seperation and arranged living conditions, she could not truly find where to place the fault. The fault did not fall on her sisters, brother, or even her. Yet she accepted the responsibility of her parents irresponsibilty. She believed she was held accountable for their actions and inactions. Sarah absorbed every inch of her situation and manifested it as if it was all her fault. How? How could her dad walking out and her mom's mental illness be her fault? She didn't know the answer, but Sarah was convinced she was just hiding it from hersself and others.

Sarah always saw life hard and unsuccessful for her but so easy for her siblings. She told herself repeatedly that her siblings have it hard just like her, but for some reason, she could not bring herself to believe that statement no matter how many times she told it to herself. Sarah siblings made the struggle look good. When was success going to visit her life and flip it upside down? When was she going to come up in life? Sarah's self-confidence was delayed in its formation. She longed for positivity, held on to it until her fingers felt slippery, but negativity was always there to pour soap on her hands. Every time positive came, negative showed up to knock it down.

How could she deal with the pain tormenting her? She began shifting the pain and the anger back and forth. Her anger shifted from resenting her family, to self-hating, and self-harming. Sarah even became furious with herself for being unable to control it all. She was upset with the way her life was turning out. Instantly, Sarah realized that her mother's afflictions not only affected her life but it created unmovable stains on the life of her daughter. Sarah thought to herself that a curse must have been put on her family's life, she felt as though she could not escape the curse but by death. She began contemplating suicide she refused to sit silent and suffer, to see her mother suffer.

Chapter 2

Each year in the United States more than 34,000 people

commit suicide

Sarah was only 15 years old when she decided life wasn't worth battling. Late one-night Sarah went into her sister's bathroom, looked for the tool that would put her into a deep sleep, and found four pills that were formulated for nighttime cold and flu. Sarah just knew those would do the trick, she would go to sleep and remain there forever. She anxiously waited for that rest to come, but death never came to deliver. She was confident that death would deliver her from her personal agony. Sarah just knew peace was hers. Peace and a death she longed for, never came, but her food sure did. Sarah vomited profusely as if she had eaten bad cheese. She threw up from the meds she had ingested.

Her sister came quickly into the room and she knew something was wrong. Shaniece rushed her sister to the hospital, where they kept Sarah for a couple of hours just to observe her.

The doctors informed them that the amount of meds Sarah took in were only enough to upset her stomach and cause vomiting. Sarah thought, "Wow, I can't even succeed at killing myself." It wasn't over because they said it was, Sarah's stomach settled down, but her mind began to erupt all over again. This time it was worse than before. Her days after the hospital were unbearable and she counted down for the next attempt. Sarah sadness turned vicious and she turned on everyone even herself.

She had more and more desires of suicide that happened by long, peaceful, and never-ending naps. Suicide was her only way out. She, had to attempt it again with hopes to get it right this time. Her next tool of choice was a drug she felt could do a better job. She even ingested 11 of them versus the 4 she took the last time. This had to worked, she had to go out with this method. Her story didn't come to an end so she tried cutting her wrist. "Still a failure, I can't find a great place in my thoughts, I can't find a great place on earth, now I can't even find a great place in death."

Unfortunately, her attempts landed her in a mental facility. The hospital admitted Sarah against her will and she had no say so, if she would go or stay. Her home for the week would be in the Cajun city of New Orleans, at Riverdale Hospital.

Mental Institutions are to treat acute psychological illness, dual diagnosis, trauma-based disorders, compulsive behaviors, and eating disorders.

Sarah dreaded knowing she would be in a "Crazy house" for an entire week. "I guess I am officially crazy now!", she said, while in route to the hospital. The security guard looked at her puzzled, as if he thought she knew her diagnosis already. He replied "Baby everybody needs some help some time, you will leave this place a changed person." Sarah looked up at the guard who seemed to be at least 6 feet tall, with a sharp haircut, buttered skin, crisp uniform, and real buff arms. "Easy for you to say sir, when you're not the one going to be locked down in a crazy house!" As they exited the vehicle and entered the building, Sarah heart raced, her legs literally shook as if they were on a moutain of snow waiting to ski to the bottom. The guard walked Sarah down the big white halls, he didn't say a word of comfort, he was leading her to the place that would create a record that could never be erased. At the nurse's station, a thin white lady with slinky curly hair, nude lipstick, nude eye shadow, but hot pink nail polish, looked up at Sarah. "Nice to meet you", I'm Tandy, we are glad to have you." Sarah disgusted by what she thought was sarcasm replied, "Well ma'am, unfortunately, I am not glad to be here or meet you, so just prescribe my stupid medication so I can get out of your face and this place." The nurse gave Sarah a slight smile and her big hazel eyes pieced through the hard-shell Sarah had been molding in her defense. "Let's get through the necessities then we take a walk."

The nurse took Sarah's vital signs, explained a few rules, and directed her to her room. Unexpectedly, Sarah had a roommate. Her name was Alice and she truly wore her name. Alice had real pretty long blonde hair, she was a bit on the chubby side, but showed up really pretty as soon as Sarah walked through the door. Excitedly, Alice walked up to Sarah and quickly reached her hand out for a shake. Sarah stood there for a minute wondering who pulled this chubby chick from the box where the Jack In The Box should have been? Maybe its what she needed. Sarah then reached out her hand to greet Alice.

"I'm sorry, my name is Sarah, this isn't easy for me, excuse me, I have to put my things down and go to the restroom", Sarah said hurriedly and frantically moving pass smiling Alice. Alice all teeth and pinkly cheeks replied, "Sure, make yourself comfortable.". After Sarah came from the bathroom, Alice insisted on telling Sarah the do's and don'ts of the facility. "So", Alice said in a hesitant voice,"No eating in the room, no sleeping after five a.m, no cell phones, we can only make phone calls at 10:00a.m. and 8 p.m., we have to attend therapeutic sessions four times a day, and…" Sarah rolled her eyes and cut off what Alice was about to say. "All of this is unnecessary, how is any of this supposed to be change or a benefit to me?". There is only one solution to the problems I'm having, and it isn't therapeutic sessions. If I can get my parents to be involved in my life, everything would be so much better.

Alice looked at Sarah with a hope that she could agree with her, Alice touched Sarah on the shoulder, and before walking out the door she said, "I wish you the best, good luck, I'm going to sit in the commons area and watch cartoons." Sarah shouted "Are you kidding me? They are making me, a 15-year-old, watch cartoons? Sarah slung herself to her bed, put her face in a pillow, and began to cry her eyes out. Sarah cried so long, she fell asleep in the wet pool of tears on her new but used pillow- cased pillow.

As the days went by Sarah's experience at the hospital was not that bad as she expected. She actually started to have a peace of mind. She didn't know if it was being isolated from her world problems, or if it was the 10 mg Prozac they started her on. Whatever it was, her thoughts had finally calmed down, and she was able to think straight.

Sarah attended several counseling sessions. Each day she opened up bit by bit. She was hoping that somehow, someway this would help her deal with life when she was discharged. She even thought the friendship she was forming with Alice would turn into something great. They were turning into the best of friends. They sat together for breakfast, lunch, and dinner. Even when the lights went off, they stayed up talking about their deepest darkest secrets. Sarah felt comfortable around Alice, she wanted her opinion about almost everything. "Do you actually think this place will make us better Alice? I have two days until I'm released, and I'm scared of facing the world again.", Sarah hoping to get a wise answer, but never waited on Alice's response. "I think my family will see me differently. They may think I'm an actress or someone seeking attention, but honestly my heart literally aches me." Alice looked over at her new friend and said, "I really don't know Sarah, but if it doesn't work for me, Ima fake it til I make it! I will be damned if they ship me back to this place again!" Sarah and Alice laughed hard while telling each other to "Shhh" so they wouldn't wake the other patients. "Good night Alice.", "Good night Sarah."

The very last day at the hospital Sarah was scheduled for a family conference. As Sarah began to get dressed her name was called for her family meeting. She quickly threw on a pink shirt and some wrinkle jeans "Well I hope they aren't expecting me to look decent. I am in a mental hospital without an iron.", Sarah mumbled to herself.

By the time she made it to the door, her hands were sweaty, and so was the rest of her body. She had not seen her sister in a whole week, and now she has to explain to her big sister why she repeatedly attempted to suicide. Sarah clutched the doorknob with her sweaty hands and waited a minute to catch her breath. Anxiety was trying to set in but she couldn't go in all confused and panicky. She took a deep breath "Just relax, nothing else could go wrong from here. You're already in a mental institution for GOD sake!" Sarah pleaded to herself.

"Sarah Jenkins, your family is waiting in the family room. Please report to the family room." The nurse's voice came over the intercom in a very loud sarcastic way. "Oh, shut up, I'm going in, I'm going!" Sarah shouted loudly while facing the intercom that was in the corner of the ceiling, by the conference room door. It was if the nurse could see Sarah standing there scared to enter the room. Anxiously, she walked in, and there was her sister and brother-n-law sitting in the right corner of the room. They seemed delighted to see her, she wasn't expecting delight. The psychiatrist sat on the other side of the room at a table filled with pictures of other patients who left with their loving families.

As Sarah slowly sat down, she noticed Shanice and James reaching into a big pink bag, tasseled with ribbon that held up 6, huge mylar balloons. How did she miss those balloons? they were so joyful, swaying back and forth against the air blowing from the ceiling fan. They took away the anxiety she was feeling and now she could see the colors of the beautiful pajamas sets they bought for her. They pulled out different color polka dots, pretty pink shirts, and fun matching socks. She felt ready, she thought she was ready, but the feeling left when she heard the doctor speak.

"Sarah, have a seat." The doctor said with a smile. "Sarah, can you tell me about the people in your family conference today"? Yes, that's my sister Shanice and her husband, James. Shanice looked at Sarah and smiled. "I love them.", she said to the doctor. She turned her entire body towards them and said, "I love you guys so much but sometimes I get really sad." With empathy her sister asked, "Well, why are you sad Sarah?" Sarah held her head down because she couldn't bring herself to tell the honest truth. She couldn't bear seeing her sister's disappointment or maybe she would be relieved because she was feeling the same way. Either way, Sarah was scared to see Shanice's reaction.

She kept her head down and whispered, "I don't know, I just am." The doctor chimed in, "Tell them why you are sad Sarah, remember we talked about you being brave and honest." Sarah didn't notice that little Ms. Slinky Hair had walked in to give her support. Even though they didn't intend to get along, Sarah had taken a mysterious liken to her. The nurse gave her a smile and nodded, the nod somehow sent courage to Sarah. She put her head back down and said in a very low tone," It's not because of anything you all did wrong. I just need my biological parents, and that's something not even you can give me." Sarah boldly picked her head up to see their expressions. They were tearful, she was shocked, she didn't know what to feel.

Shanice, tears running down her face, replied "Well, I know we're not mama or George, but we are trying to be the best parents we can be to you and Patrick." James nodded his head in agreement, with tears falling, and his legs shaky. His voice trembling, he said, "You can even call me dad if you want. I love you like you are my own child." While their expression of love made Sarah's heart smile and gave her momentary happiness, she suddenly felt sadness because they couldn't possibly understand her heartache. Sarah was truly grateful for her sister and James. She thought Shanice was a great mother figure to them and James was an awesome father figure. Nevertheless, it didn't matter how great they were to Sarah and Patrick, they could not fill that void called orphan. They could not pour into that abandoned place she lived with.

At that moment she realized, she wasn't ready nor willing to accept love from anyone or anywhere else, if it wasn't from her parents. Thinking about her nieces and nephew stirred her up even more. Sarah wanted to enjoy life, she wanted to accept the gifts and balloon, she wanted to just be happy. She couldn't, her pain, sorrow, and depression didn't allow it. She was slowly slipping back into that unforgettable place. How would she make them understand? She loved them, but right now she wished her mom had bought those balloons, those pajamas for a sleepover that she would be taking her to, or the socks to slip and slide in. Right now, the only people she wanted to talk to were her parents.

She wanted a real bond with them, not with her sister, brother-n-law, neices, or nephew. Her battle was against mental illness, it was the culprit keeping her and her mother seperated. It was the reason her smile begin turning into a frown right before their faces. The disconnect was a real party pooper for her.

Anything that looked like love or felt like love, Sarah built up a wall and blocked it out. "Sarah, Sarah, did you hear me? If you ever find yourself wanting to take your life, what are you going to do differently?", her sister asked as if she had said it more than once. "I will call the 1-800-suicide hotline or reach out to a loved one. "Well there you have it, Sarah I think you are ready to go home." the doctor said those words with a big smile, contrary to what Sarah felt." I can't stay here forever, so I have no choice." Sarah replied with a shortened smile.

Chapter 3

As she packed up her belongings, Shanice and James waited outside for her. "I'm writing my number on the chalkboard. Whenever you are discharged, please call me.", she told Alice. Sarah started to sniffle and before she knew it, she was sobbing like a baby cub being separated from her momma bear." Girl, don't you start that crying! We just got to a point where we don't accept sadness anymore, remember? I will keep in touch with you Sarah, now go use some bravery in your new life. Kick butt and know that I will catch up with you later". "I love you, Alice! I will never forget about you. I couldn't have made it this week without you." "I love you too Sarah, you will be just fine."

Sarah and Alice hugged each other one last time before she left the room. She did feel the same about her family, but not the same about those long white walls she saw on her way out of that cold building. Sarah jumped in the back of James red Chevy truck and immediately took in the scent of men's cologne and Shanice's hair spritz.

The ride was a silent tour home. When they finally made it, Sarah walked into the house, and there sat her nieces and her nephew. "Please do not start asking embarassing questions.", Sarah thought to herself. Her nieces and nephew never said a word about her being away. Surprisingly, they hugged her and told her how much she was missed and loved. With a smile and shutter nerves, she responded, "I love you guys too, I am glad to be home."

Sarah seemed to live what she and her family believed to be a "stable life". She went on to do great in school and made tons of friends. She finished middle school with honors. Everything seemed to be on a wonderful rise. Her next move was high school and instead of excitement, she felt fear and anxiety. Going into the 9th grade, felt like the beginning of a new life. It would mean another change in life, that both parents would never take part in.

High school caused her life to spiral. She went from avoiding love relationships to searching for love in all of the wrong young men. She started running away and would even bike miles and miles away just to go to a friend's house. Often, she left her family nervous and scared. Many nights her sister Shanice went out to hunt for her, returning home exhausted and hopeless. Sarah adopted more problems, dabbled in trouble, and grew rebellious.

"She's not my mother, she cannot tell me what to do! Why doesn't she command her own damn children? My mama is sick and my daddy ain't nothing, and I'm grown enough. Why do I have to do what she tells me?", Sarah said while walking the street one late night. She decided that love from a man was what she needed. She needed to find someone that would love and comfort her without all of the commands. So she found her a boyfriend. "I might as well get me a boyfriend that will love me since my daddy won't!", she kept chanting to herself. Sarah's dad George was the first man ever to break her heart, and now she set out to find love that her father should have given her years ago.

She started on the hunt to replace George, what one man won't do, another one will. That's when she fell for Jonathan. He was tall, 6'2, husky, manly type, with a raspy deep voice. "I'm so glad I found you baby. I never thought I could be loved the right way, until I found you." She always made sure to serenade him, she didn't want to take any chance of him abandoning her. Sarah took many dream vacations in Jonathan's pretty brown eyes, wet kisses, sttrong embraces, or freeing smile. She wished she could live in her daydreams.

Jonathan and Sarah attended the same school, so they spent a lot of time together, in and out of school. "So, do you want to skip school today and hang out by ourselves?" Sarah asked and Johnathan quickly responded, "Sure! Why not, we need some alone time away from Kayla who hovers like she's my mom. They are always watching our every move!"

Not today! Sarah and Jonathan went to Kayla's house with the intent to get extra close, more kisses, and maybe rub a little. What happened was unexpected but expected. Sarah and Jonathan went into one of Kayla's rooms, and one thing led to another., Sarah lost her virginity to Jonathan. Sarah begin panicking and screaming, "OH, MY GOD! Jonathan! I'm bleeding! Am I supposed to be bleeding?" "Calm down babe, I just popped your cherry. You're not a virgin anymore." Johnathan said calmly while rubbing her chill bumped arm. "Well, at least I lost it to someone I love." "I love you too. Now, come on let's hurry back to school, fourth quarter is almost over!" Jonathan said in his heavy breathing and while kissing Sarah. They both got dressed rushed back to school. Sarah and Jonathan became inseparable.

They never went a day without spending time together. After school, they hung out from sun-up to sun-down.

Now that Sarah would be bunking with her sister, she had to find new ways to sneak and see her lover. Kayla was another older sister, and now Sarah's new, wanna- be mom. She was married to a man named Michael. Michael was blunt, straightforward, and tough. Sarah's perception of Michael was suspicious. She felt that he was too cocky. He would say exactly what he felt, at the time he felt it, and did not care if it hurt or not. He was flaming with bad vibes but she couldn't put her finger on the cause. There was something about him she just didn't like and as time went on she understood why.

They never got along. He was to the point and in your face, while Sarah was straight disrespectful and stubborn. Michael wanted everyone to believe he wore truth on his sleeve and his word was bond. Sarah didn't care anything about his word being bond or even his breath being stank. She had developed the backbone of a dinosaur and could now speak her mind with boldness. She decided that she would serve notice to anyone who needed to get it. Yes, she was still young, but her voice carried now. She would tell herself, "They can call me a smart mouth, I don't care! So what if they don't like it."

What were they going to do about her snappiness? It was really her cover for the forever hurt? If decided, they could choose to pop her in the mouth, snatch her up, or just shut up about it all. She stayed focus on getting the last word from now on. She was sick and tired of being abandoned, overlooked, and silenced. Now, as if she transformed into a giant, she would always have a verbal comeback for the slick talkers. They were done getting over on her mentally, verbally, and physically. Sarah was growing up.

Well, since my daddy didn't want to love me, I got me a man who does." Sarah told herself this while daydreaming about her Johnathan. He was so loving and kind, so was his family. They welcomed Sarah with open arms, she could visit anytime she wanted.

One sunny morning, Sarah and Jonathan were chilling in his room, talking and laughing. Jonathan had the spirit of an old wise man. He even had older friends, one of them named Leroy. Leroy was around the age of 25 at the time, married, with children. Jonathan and Leroy would chill and talk at Leroy's house on a week to week basis. He lived near, right up the street, walking distance. "Hey, you know the dude Leroy who I be chillin with?" "Yes, why what's up, what about him?" Sarah replied. "His wife looks identical to you! She really does have the same skin tone as you. Your eyes, mouth, and the nose are very similar." "Oh okay, that's weird", Sarah brushed it off. "Seriously, I think I found your sister. I even think your dad be at her house from time to time."

Jonathan knew how Sarah's dad looked because he would pop up at Kayla's house every now and then. When he did, Jonathan just so happened to be there. Sarah looked at Jonathan like he was crazy. "Babe really? Now you're starting to sound crazy and you know that's absurd! You

know I only have three sisters and they're by my mom.",

Sarah said while laughing. "Maybe I am crazy, maybe I'm

not, it won't hurt to just go ask the lady who her daddy is."

Jonathan looked at Sarah with a serious expression.

"Okay babe! I will do it just for you." Jonathan softly, kissed

Sarah on the lips, "Now get up and go see! Leroy's wife

usually gets home from work around this time." "Okay, I'm

going now, but if you're wrong, you owe me something

special." Sarah jumped off the bed and headed towards

Leroy's house. Jonathan was confident this woman was

related to Sarah in some way. He knew she could be her

sister, aunt, or a cousin.

Sarah arrived at the park across from Leroy and his

wife's house. "I'm going to sit at this park across the street

from their house. I have to see this lady before I let Jonathan

make assumptions." Sarah said to herself while nervously

shaking her head. "This boy got me out here looking like a

freaking stalker", she mumbled to herself as if someone was watching to see if she was delusional. Sarah, shaking uncontrollably from nervousness, stared across the street as Leroy's wife pulled into the driveway. She got out of the car with her three kids following, begin unloading her groceries, and headed toward the house. Sarah slowly combed every inch of the woman's face. She could not stop staring because to her surprise, Jonathan wasn't lying.

Her face reminded Sarah of how beautiful she was, a great reflection of herself. She was the spitting image of Sarah. "This is insane! This has to be an aunt I've never met, a long-lost cousin, or someone kin!" Sarah could not move, she just sat there contemplating if she should find out the truth or leave it alone. How could this lady be related to her? Leroy's wife suddenly noticed Sarah watching her. "WHAT ARE YOU LOOKING AT LITTLE GIRL?" ARE YOU ONE OF MY HUSBAND'S SIDELINES OR SOMETHING?", his wife yelled. Sarah quickly turned her head and walked further into the park. She sat on a bench

panicking, "Sarah get up and go ask her, if not this lady may

think you're a psycho, side chick, who followed her husband

home. Use your courage, be brave." Alice's words replayed

in Sarah head like a tape recording. Sarah got up and slowly

walked to Leroy's house. Sarah knocked once. His wife must

have been watching her walk over and was probably just as

curious as Sarah was to find out who this mysterious girl

was.

She swung the door open with an attitude and

snapped, "May I help you?" Sarah looked at her and quietly

answered, "Ma'am, I think you are my half-sister, we might

have the same dad." "Baby, I don't have a sister, I have four

brothers. What's your name and who is your dad?" "My

name is Sarah. My dad's name is George", Sarah replied.

After a long awkward pause, she looked at Sarah with tears

in her eyes, and quickly grabbed her phone to call her dad.

She shouted through the mouth piece, "DADDY! DO YOU

HAVE SOMETHING TO TELL ME?" Sarah watched as she

held the phone in disbelief. Her face lost its color as if she

had seen a ghost. "YES, Marie I didn't tell you and your

brothers, that you have a baby sister named Sarah and two

brothers named Patrick and Dedrick .", their father answered

in a apologetic voice, at least it seemed that way coming over

the speaker phone. "Well, I knew about Patrick but you never

told me I had a sister and another brother. Daddy, you were

here two hours ago, why did you hide my only sister from

me? Why did you hide my brother?" "I didn't know how to

tell you, Marie, please don't be mad at me.", he answered in a

low voice as if shame had covered his face, especially his

mouth. "Well too late for that, I can't believe you!" Marie

hung up the phone.

Marie hugged Sarah with a hug so tight, her tiny

frame could crumble upon release. "How could my daddy

walk out my life, live in the same city as me, and then have

the nerve to keep his children apart. OH! He got him some

nerves!" Sarah thought to herself. She went back and forward, forward and back, trying to find an explanation for him. How could he be involved in their life and abandon us like lost trinkets. "Dirty bastard!" She mumbled under her breath

"Hey kids come in here! You have an aunt I would like you to meet", Marie shouted to the back. Marie's kids came running to into the living room. Her three boys were all very handsome and each one gave Sarah a big hug. Marie picked her phone up and dialed out, she was excited to spread the news. "Hey, come over here, I have someone I want you to meet." Then with a puzzled look on her face, she asked, "So, your other sisters never mentioned anything about us to you?" "Uh, no. I mean not unless they told me when I was younger, and I just don't remember it." Sarah responded.

"Well, your sisters know me. We have always been kind of close to one another. I am surprised that she never mentioned you to me. I knew about Patrick but not you.

Sarah sat speechless, just nodding and shaking her head. Suddenly, a knock at the door startled the silence, and Marie jumped up excitedly. "Just sit here for a second", Marie said. I wonder who that is? What else could possibly be added to this mess?", Sarah whispered, she was becoming overwhelmed.

Two men walked in the door, "Rodney and David", Marie turned to Sarah, "I would like to introduce you to our baby sister, Sarah." "Stop playing Marie, whose child do you have?" Rodney and David laughed. "I'm not playing with you, I'm serious, call daddy and ask him!" "Let me be the first to make that call.", Rodney said while laughing and calling his dad's number at the same time. "Daddy is it true that you have other kids besides us and Patrick? You only told us about Patrick, why wouldn't you tell us about the others?"

"I'm sorry son but it's true." "Are you kidding me dad, why would you keep your kids a secret. I missed out on so many years of their life because of you." Rodney, David, and Marie met Patrick before Sarah was born, but didn't see him again until years later. Rodney hung the phone up. Sarah sat there in shock the entire time not uttering a word. "What the hell is going on? This is some soap opera type stuff, this can't be real life." Sarah thought to herself. As she looked at the new faces of her siblings, she noticed their facial features were very similar to hers. "So where are our brothers, where do they live, we want to meet them."

"My sister Shanice are raising me and Patrick, my other sister are raising Dedrick." OK, we will go see them tomorrow." "I love you little sister, take care, and call me if you need anything." Rodney said. Sarah stood up and gave each of her siblings a hug and kiss on the cheek, "It's nice meeting you all, but I have to get home or Shanice will start looking for me. It's getting dark." "I cannot believe all of this! All of this time I wished I had a sister and I actually have one. This is awesome man!", said Marie! "Love you little sister keep my number and you can call or come by anytime."

"Thank you, and I will most definitely keep in touch, we have some catching up to do". Sarah walked at a really fast pace, as she headed down the street to tell Jonathan all about the journey he sent her on. When she made it to his house, she bust through front door, and flew by everybody in the house to get to Jonathan. "Girl, you better had won the lottery busting in here like that." Jonathan's mother shouted in a joking manner.

"Babe, you would never believe it, well maybe you would." Sarah shouted to Jonathan. "Well don't waste time Sarah, tell me already, was I right?" " Oh my God! Yes, you were babe, you were right. Leroy's wife, Marie is my sister just like you figured." "Get out of here! I told you babe!" Jonathan said excitedly, he even stood up and did a corny hi-five. Sarah burst into laughter while trying to tell him more about the story. "How about I have two older brothers, their names are Rodney and David." "Wait what? There are more of you?" Jonathan started anxiously pacing his room floor and shaking his head in disbelief.

"Yes, I have three siblings I never knew about and George didn't tell any of us about the other. They knew about Patrick but had no clue about me and my brother Dedrick. "Wow!", Jonathan said with his mouth opened wide. "That's some real crazy tv like stuff babe. How are you feeling about all of this?" "At this point, I'm not sure how to feel or what to think. I need some time to process it all, but it's getting late babe, I have to be back to Kayla's house before she rats on me to Shanice." Johnathan kissed Sarah and hugged her in tight. He knew she needed to feel love and wanted. "Okay babe, I love you, call me first thing in the morning."

Sarah finally made it to Kayla's house and eventually Shanice was there to get her. She calmly got into the car and minutes later, thoughts of deception, lies, and manipulation began to swarm her mind. Why didn't they tell us we had other siblings? Did they tell me when I was young and I just don't remember?" That could possibly be an explanation for it, but I'm 16 now and they still haven't opened up to me about it. Her mind was riddled with questions that she felt needed to be answered now. She couldn't help but replay over and over, "Oh my GOD, in less than 24 hours I have a new branch of family, this has to be a dream."

She thought about those occasions when she visited her aunt on her dad's side. Even then, it wasn't mentioned. It was as if that information wasn't important enough for her to know. She finally convinced herself of sleep, "I have to get some rest before my mind blows up with curiosity." The following day, Sarah refuse to hold the ice water any longer. With a slight eye roll and snappy tone, Sarah blurted, "Shanice I found my other sister and brothers. So how come, over the years, you all never mentioned anything about them?" "Girl! We did tell yall, maybe you just don't remember, I mean it was a while ago.", Shanice answered

Sarah without even looking her direction. She said it with confidence, like it was truth.

That's about as far as the conversation went. Sarah took her sister's word for it and didn't dig any deeper. She was emotionally drained and had no more room to process drama or secrets. The drama she had just experienced was enough to carry her into the summer. She was now out of school for almost three months and was faced with a serious decision. As much as she wanted to be excited about all of the extra time with Jonathan, she wanted to spend more time finding the missing pieces of her life. She had hoped to put the pieces back together. Spending her time with her boyfriend sounded great but who was she kidding, they probably wouldn't even marry in the next decade.

"I'm sorry Jonathan. I think we need a break.", Sarah told Jonathan over the phone. "Okay, baby girl. I don't want to hold you up, I understand you have a lot going on in your life. I don't want to be a distraction. Whatever you're looking for, I hope you find it and have peace with it. We are still young, so who knows what the future holds for us." Jonathan said in a somewhat hopeful tone. "Thank you for understanding Jonathan, see you around babe!"

Summertime brought hang time. Shanice let Sarah spend weekends over at her sister Marie's house. Everytime she went expecting to see her dad. He never came around, and while Sarah loved spending time with her siblings, she really wanted the scoop on her daddy's absence. What was keeping him away? What kept him away over the years. She would get free from her thoughts when she played with her nephews. She had grown close to them and they had become a huge part of Sarah's world.

Sarah didn't have money but she was sure to spoil them with love, time and attention. Some days Sarah wanted to feel complete with her newfound family, but she knew that was only one of many pieces to her puzzle.

Chapter 4

Sarah became her own woman and things got heated between her and Shanice. One day they got into a heated argument that drove Sarah out of the house. She left there to go live with another one of her older sisters. Candace was the baby girl before Sarah was born. There was always a little tension because of it but nothing that would keep them from being able to live together.

The mental sickness her mom suffered with did not allow for her to live alone. Candace was taking care of their mom at the time Sarah moved in. Sarah was so excited to be under the same roof as her mom. Unfortunately, they were still out of touch. The schizophrenia took her mom out of the real world. Sarah wanted dearly to develop and grow a relationship with her mom but many days she would find that her mom left the room, without leaving the room. It was tough on her. Some days they could talk like it was real life and on other days her mom would mentally disappear.

Sarah was learning to accept those awkward moments, silent times, and unrealistic moments she would experience when being around her mom. She wanted to have regular conversations, share her feelings, laugh and shower her mom with jokes, but it never happened. Sarah started to embrace the small moments she had with her mom. "My little bit of girl, hey mama baby!" Sarah's mom would always say the same thing whenever she passed by her bedroom door. "Hey mommie", Sarah would always reply. Those were the times she would have to hang tight to and cherish because her stay there would not be long.

"My mom has never had an easy life, why is that?", Sarah questioned herself time and time again. What happened, why did she get sick, what cause her to lose grip of real life? No matter how many times she asked or how many days she wondered, her siblings stuck with the story.

Her mom's illness separated her from her children. She was getting sicker and it took away her ability to raise Sarah, Patrick, and Dedrick.

Still she just could not shake it. It was like a scary movie she watched that would keep her from sleeping at night. Thoughts were like haunting nightmares. "Things are not adding up, how could she all of a sudden get sick and unable to raise her children? There are three of us, one and two years apart! It just doesn't make sense!", Sarah argued with herself. She knew her mom was sick, that was the truth, but their timeline sounded a wee bit fishy. She believed when her mother gave birth to her, Patrick, and Dedrick she was absolutely sane. So, what the heck happened? What went wrong that took her over the edge? Sarah was destined to find out even though a small part of her felt like she would never know. She even went on an information hunt asking several of her family members and everyone had a different answer.

Many of them confessed her mother's sanity, saying she was well when she gave birth to them. Through the eyes of some family members, she got a glimpse of who her mom was. They described her as really quiet, some said she was one of the sweetest ladies on the earth. The talked about her kind heart, long talks, and even her long pretty hair. Even though she was known for being quiet, she would spark up a conversation if you gave her a drink. Despite all that she heard happened, good and bad, she loved her mom deeply. Therefore, she could not leave well enough alone. The family grew impatient with Sarah.

Every action and inaction of Sarah was based on her inability to settle with the situation of her youth. She drove family away because she wanted truth. They eventually stopped reaching out to Sarah. Those feelings of abandonment sprung from almost everyone she was connected to. She was like the outcast. They no longer wanted her to be around, they pushed at her every move to be loved. At least that is what she thought they were doing to her. They labeled her "needy" and eventually grew tired of her depending on them. No one stopped to ask Sarah what was driving her? They didn't ask what steps she had already taken to help her deal with the stress. No one saw if progress had come or could come. Everyone just assumed she wasn't trying hard enough to keep herself from a dark place. Her life had become a chore for family and a hassle for her. It was tough just waking up each morning to face another day.

Sometimes in life, dealing with a family member who suffers from mental illness, can cause unwanted separation. If we can't help them, we tend to shut them out, or criticize them. We get tired of the same old depressing story and we assume that they don't want change. We have to realize that we are not them and therefore we cannot discern their battles. We may even feel that they are too dependent and so we shove them into independence and expect them help themselves. That is not the ideal way to handle it. They have

emotions too, one of them could be hopelessness.Could it be

that they have tried it their way and every route they take, it

comes to a dead end? Anytime we deal with a loved one who

experiences trauma, abandonment, neglect and many

hardship, we should not lose our patience. Being impatient

could leave the situation and especially the loved one in a a

position of being misunderstood. If we are not careful with

our assumptions, it could cause more trauma. 4

Statistic show 702,000 children were confirmed by child

protective services for abuse and neglections and in one long

term study as many as 80% of young adults who have been

abused or neglected, physically or mentally, meet the

diagnostic criteria for at least one mental disorder. Sarah

was a part of that 80 %. Sarah experienced depression,

anxiety, eating disorders, and even suicide attempts.

Sarah wanted her family to understand her stresses, depressions, and dark places. She wanted them to do their research, find out what could help or how they could help. Before they decided that she wasn't trying hard enough, she wanted them to consider just how hard she way trying. Sarah had no motivation and thought repeatedly," If my own family doesn't believe in me why should I? Maybe, just maybe, they're right and I'm not trying hard enough." She needed them to notice her and recognize the milestones, whether big or small.

Chapter 5

Sarah started to enjoy more time with her dad. She spent more time with her half-sister and brothers. Every time she saw them, her dad wasn't too far behind. She enjoyed her times with George. His personality was witty and humorous. Sarah started calling him the funniest man on earth. At least he was the funniest man she knew on earth at the time. He was a real comedian. There was never a dull moment around George, always being the life of the party. "Hey pop what you doing?" Sarah said to George, "Oh nothing, but you sure are ugly!", he would jokingly snap back. "Well, if I'm ugly, you're ugly too because I'm your reflection.", Sarah laughed and George laughed too as they embraced with a hug. He was starting to grow on her and she liked it. Nevertheless, she remained a skeptic of it all. She still wanted the answers due to her. Why did he sign his over his rights? Why did he neglect us? Were the stories true? Did he really beat `her mother profusely, like many people said? Was it really all George's fault? What was so different now, how is he comfortable enough to enjoy his daughter's company?

Sarah was tempted to ask every question imaginable, but she didn't. She finally felt worthy of his time and it was a wonderful feeling. Her long-lost father was back in her lifeand she didn't want to jeopardize the growing relationship. Sarah savoured every moment she got to spend with her father. The thoughts came across her mind every time she saw him, but something in her heart just wouldn't let her open up. She wanted him to know about her pain and the pain her brothers may have felt. Sarah did not give into the itch, she didn't want to take the risk of ruining what they were building.

Holding it all in begin to eat away at her. Her thoughts had come to life. Her thoughts were now so loud that they seemed to be coming from another person. "I wonder if he ever stopped to think about how much pain, suffering, and dysfunction he had caused you when he gave you up? He is such a selfish, inconsiderate bastard!", Sarah's thoughts screamed in her head. It set fire to her and she felt ready to call him out. "How can the man who first broke your heart, before any other man had the chance, just come back in your life like everything is okay?" Sarah thoughts were questioning her and George. Sarah answered, "I guess I am supposed to act as if he did nothing wrong." Somehow Sarah's love for her father always prevailed over her thoughts. She had the right to ask but the heart to leave it alone. Sarah was getting what she always wanted from George, acceptance. He could possibly show her enough love now that would heal her broken heart. She was willing to wait until her courage caught up with her thoughts.

Sarah's mental health began to deteriorate right before her eyes; she grew tired and weary from moving all of the time. She was going from pillow to post, after wearing out her welcome at her family members houses. Now she was always looking for sleep. Sarah wanted to take sleeping pills all throughout the day so she could sleep and avoid waking up to deal with life troubles. It had become much easier for her to cry than laugh.

Sarah prayed, "God I'm so tired, what am I here for? What's my purpose? Nobody even cares about me, they don't care if I live or die. Why can't you just call me home Lord, I'm not wanted here on earth.", Sarah buried her head in a pillow, crying out to the Lord. She put up a fight against death. Sarah fought against suicidal thoughts and self-harm, it became a daily ritual. Nobody knew and nobody cared, they never even cared to ask.

Sarah began to cry out on social media, expressing her emotions. Luckily, one of her old middle school friends saw her cry for help. Her old friend wrote her in her private message," Sarah are you okay"? Sarah hesitated to respond, she realized she was too embarrassed to tell her the details. How could she tell her that she was homeless? "Maybe I should write her back. Maybe that's what I need, a friend to help me through hard times." She hyped herself up enough to finally respond. "I am not okay Bee, I'm going from house to house. I am staying with my half-brother right now but I don't know how long that's going to last. Everyone is always getting tired of me staying with them.'"" Sarah where does your brother stay?" Bee asked excitedly! "His house is on Midway Avenue, in the 70805 zip code." "OMG, you are like 10 minutes away from me! Do you want to meet me halfway? We can chill by my mom's house tonight, she won't mind at all?" "YES!", Sarah typed all caps and shouted at the computer as if Bee could hear her. Sarah immediately messaged Bee again. "I would love that, I wouldn't mind a girl's night. It might actually help take my mind off of everything. "Cool! Meet me at the Renaissance Center on the corner of Plank Road." "Ok, I'm on my way right now!" Sarah quickly grabbed her nikes, shoved them on her feet, and took off walking towards their meting spot. Sarah walked for almost five miles to meet Bee. They arrived at the same time. "Omg girl! I missed you!", Bee said with a big smile while hugging Sarah. Bee had the same pretty brown skin like Sarah remembered and those model like facial features. She was a pretty girl, well-dressed, brand name clothes and shoes, matching accessories, black girl fine like they say, and really pretty long, jet black hair.

"She looks like she had a good life", Sarah thought to herself while responding to Bee," I missed you to girl. So are you sure your mom is not going to have a problem with me spending the night?" Sarah was nervous. "Girl no! I have the coolest mom, she actually loves all of my friends. You will see, come on let's go to the house. It gets hectic on Plank Road at night, and I don't want anything to do with it." Sarah knew exactly what Bee meant by that statement. Plank Road at night would bring out the transexuals, homosexuals, and prostitutes. Plank Road was very dangerous for any teenager so they most definitely should not be out nightfall

Bee and Sarah headed to Bee's mother house." We finally made it girl. Come on Sarah so we can shower.", Bee said while huffing and puffing. They were both hot and sweaty from the walk. "Okay, but I have to tell you something first.", Sarah put her head down while whispering to Bee, "I don't have any underwear." Bee quickly answered and reassured Sarah, "Girl that's fine! I have brand new underwear in my closet that's never been open." My mom buy us underwear every week and it just piles up." "I wish my mom was able to do that for me.", Sarah whispered sadly. "Where is your mom?", Bee asked looking confused. "One of my older sisters take care of her. My mother is Schizophrenic. She's been like that all of my life." "Oh Ok, I'm sorry Sarah I shouldn't have asked." "No, you didn't say anything wrong. I'm used to it now, it has become my truth.", Sarah replied. "Okay well, we are not going to be sad today. Go shower we are about to have some fun.", Bee said while handing Sarah her new underwear. Sarah went to take her a nice hot shower. She stayed in the shower for almost an hour." "Knock! Knock! Hey baby, are you okay in there?", Bee's mother asked. She had made it home. "Yes ma'am, I'm getting out now.", Sarah shouted from the shower. "Ok, I'm just making sure, no rush.", her mom shouted back. The shower felt so good to Sarah she didn't want to get out. It relaxed her and she like how clean she felt after a long day. She went into Bee's room, "I'm done, all clean now girl." "Ok, I'm going now. You can watch whatever you want on TV until I get out." Bee threw Sarah the remote and left to take her shower.

Sarah laid in Bee's bed and flipped through the channels. She started thinking, "Man, this bed is really cozy and soft. This house is so well decorated, with all of the best furniture. It feels like a home in here. Bee and her siblings are really blessed." Finally, Bee got out the shower. "So, what do you want to do?", Bee asked Sarah. "How about we just catch up and talk about the old days.", Sarah said

excitedly.

They stayed up late laughing and talking the entire

time. "Girl why, one day I relaxed and dyed my hair light

blonde. I woke up the next morning and I had nothing but a

couple of strands of hair on my head!" Sarah was sharing an

embarrassing moment but it made them both laugh. Oh my

God! You are kidding, did you go to school like that?", Bee

asked while crying laughing. "Girl yes! I covered it with

weave and went to school. When I got home, my older niece

glued braids on my head, I was just that bald!" By this time,

they were screaming laughing. They were rolling all over the

bed, they could not contain the laughter. "Well I bet you

won't use that combination again?", Bee said while her eyes

were filled of tears from laughter.

They had been screaming laughing so loud that

eventually her mother woke up in the middle of the night.

Her mom's name was Ms.Pam. Ms. Pam walked into the

room and saw how much fun Bee and Sarah were having.

"Where do you stay baby?", Ms Pam asked while squinting

her eyes from the light in Bee's bedroom. Before Sarah could

answer. Bee jumped up. "Mom she doesn't have anywhere to

stay right now. She has been back and forth between her

siblings. She is staying with her brother right now, but she

never feels comfortable staying for a long time." Ms Pam's

eyes grew wider and she stood there for a minute. She then

turned to the girls and said, "Well, this is your new home

now. Go get your clothes from your brother house

tomorrow." Sarah slowly responded, "Ms Pam, I have moved

so much over the past year, I don't have too many clothes. I

left them behind over the course of time." "Well, I guess we

will have to go shopping.", Ms.Pam said while smiling. Bee

and Sarah jumped up hugging each other and screaming.

Sarah was overjoyed and super excited.

Girl I have the best taste, I'm going to make sure

you're straight. You're going to be fly!", Bee said. "OK! Go to bed girls. Tomorrow when I get off from work, we have a long day ahead of us.", Ms. pam said yawning at the same time. The girls fell asleep. The next day was a bright Saturday morning. They were so excited they got dressed early and waited around for Ms. Pam to honk her horn. That was the signal to come outside. Then, HONK! HONKKK! "Come on Sarah, Mama is outside", Bee said excitedly!.They flew out of the door.

"Seat belts please!", Ms. Pam said while looking in her rear-view mirror. Sarah and Bee buckled up and they all headed to the mall. While shopping, someone asked Ms. Pam, "Are those your girls? They look just like you." "Well this one is my adopted child." while placing her hand on Sarah shoulder smiling, and I actually have two biological daughters. "Oh, well ma'am you have some beautiful girls.", "Thank you!", she said. Sarah was so thankful she now had plenty of socks, a pair of shoes, hygiene products, a new touch screen phone, and several outfits with jewelry to match. The girls picked out matching outfits so they could dress alike. She felt that her life was changing. Her hair was growing, her nails were healthier, her face was even plumper.

Sarah enjoyed being a part of their family, they were inseparable. However, Sarah would miss her family a great deal so sshe would call them. She wanted to assure them she was safe and in good care. Sarah was happy with her new family because she could feel the presence of love with them. What she didn't expect, showed up, and overwhelmed her. Her sadness overtook her but she wondered how it got in. How could she feel sad in such a great place?

After only a couple of months started to have crying spells and depression slowly crept up once again. One day, during a spell, Ms. Pam walked into the front room and found her sobbing. Being as comforting as a mother, she sat down next to Sarah, and asked only one question; "How can I help you baby?"

Sarah responded shakenly, "Every time I want to be happy I think about why I'm not. Why can't I feel joy and love like this when I'm with my biological family?" She broke down more and more after every word she spoke. "Baby one day you are going to be better than you are today. You will be successful and your family will one day realize, you are a blessing to the family. I'm pretty sure your family loves you but some people just don't know how to show it. They may have missed showing you love and kindness but don't let that be your focus. You just focus on your ability to have happiness and it will attract the right situations to bring you just that. God is going to use you to bless a lot of people Sarah. You have to be strong and let Him make your enemies your foot stool. (Psalms 110:1) Now get you some rest."

Sarah eventually went to bed but woke up with a heavy mind. She remembered the words Ms. Pam told her but didn't totally believe it. Those words offered but a glimpse of hope and gave Sarah some small amount of faith.

Ms. Pam and the girls had been a huge comfort to Sarah. One thing was for sure. Sarah and Bee would remain true and loyal to each other. They were there for one another, going through situations together. They cried together, laughed together, and shared each other's deepest darkest secrets. Bee was the sister Sarah always wanted. Sarah and her biological sisters were almost 10 years apart. She didn't grow up with her sisters, her sister raised her. Therefore, Bee became Sarah's sister from another mother.

There came a time when, Bee could see straight through Sarah's fake smiles and false joy. She knew when Sarah was bothered and when she was really doing okay. Sarah became transparent to Bee. Bee would acknowledge Sarah's pain and accept it. She never judged or looked at her differently because of her episodes of anxiety or depression. Bee never discredited her feelings, when Sarah would have a bad day; Bee knew hugs would mean a lot in that time. Eventually, she could not comfort her sister, her friend. Bee could not get in the place where she once was because Sarah felt that is wasn't Bee's responsibility. She didn't owe her love, protection, security, and restoration. Her mother and especially her Father George were the ones that owed her.

Sarah went on the hunt for George and what he owed her. George had some explaining to do and time replacement to fulfill. Sarah made up in her mind that she would confront George whether he liked it or not. It was time that george be the father he should have been to Sarah. Sarah wasn't willing to accept love from anyone else. It was his time to step up. "My mother didn't have a chance to raise me but you did, and now it's time you prove yourself worthy of being called dad." Sarah said to herself.

Chapter 6

The Next day came. Sarah talked with Bee about her plans to reach out to her dad and possibly go live with him. Bee thought it was worth giving a shot so Sarah could get closure. After calling around, Sarah finally got a hold to George. "Hey pops this is Sarah, I need to come crash at your house for a couple of months until I get on my feet." You can come baby girl but I want you to know, my girlfriend lives here too. It won't be a problem at all, you can even have your own room.

"Cool I'm on my way. Sarah told Bee and Ms. Pam her plans. Sarah packed up, and Ms. Pam dropped Sarah off to George's house. The girls hugged each other tight. "You know, since I have my own room, you can always come spend the night by my house.", Sarah said, "You know I'm going to be over here all the time girl, this is not the end of us.

Sisters for life, right? Bee said while hugging Sarah tight. "And you already know! Ain't no separating us. Sister for life!" Sarah said while releasing bee from a hug. The first day being at george house went smoothly for Sarah as she stayed in her room the majority of the day to collect her thoughts. Sarah has yet to know what journey staying with george would take her on, but she was willing to risk her sanity to find out the truth behind her father careless actions. Sarah next morning was a little bit bizarre.

Sarah was called out for breakfast by George girlfriend, Jane "Sarah come out and eat this food! you already walking around looking like a racehorse." Sarah walked up to George girlfriend Jane and snatched the plate out of her hand. ." you know you are not too cute yourself right Jane?" Sarah said with a smirk on her face while heading to sit down and eat." you not lying either daughter, that is one ugly son of a gun, every time I turn over I think a demon on the side of me, but it's her ugliness laying on the side of me, that's one ugly woman, but I love her ugly self though" George and Sarah laughed. "Oh, hush up George you with me, so I can't be too ugly."

Jane said in a strong tone. "The devil is a lie I'm with you because I love you but you ugly as hell Jane," George said while falling out laughing. "Okay daddy now you are being just too mean. Sarah said while her face turning red from holding back her laughter. Jane sat there rolling her eyes at George while flipping the bird at him the whole time. Sarah began to eat her breakfast, as Sarah watched TV and ate her food she looked over and saw George gulping down a 40-ounce beer without even eating his food, he began to pop open beers back to back.

Well I guess this was a part of the problem right here "Sarah mumbled to herself. "How in the world could he swallow all of this liquor without even eating a full meal"? Sarah thought to herself." He had barely touched his breakfast." Sarah looked at Jane, and she sat there watching

George consume all this beer, As she lit cigarettes back to back. Sarah watched the people consume their body with all these toxins, they poisoned their body more than nurturing it. And it seems like it was normal for them.

Sarah watched this routine on a daily basis. "Lord what did I get myself into this time." Sarah thought to herself but it was too late for Sarah to back out and leave she might as well stay to see what else would be revealed. Sarah wanted to know the man who has caused her all this pain and suffering since the beginning of her time. One bright early morning. Sarah went to join George for breakfast and judge Judy court on television. Sarah and George watched court television every morning even if it was just in silence with laughter here and there, that was their way of bonding. George had just finished a beer; Jane took off walking to go run errands.

Every first of the month George got a social security check well over two thousand dollars. George was a retired veteran. George was never allowed to touch his money; everything was taken care of through Jane. Jane would purchase all the cigarettes and beer that George wanted. She paid the utilities and rent and after buying his cigarettes and beer Jane did whatever she pleased with the remaining of George check. As Sarah is sitting in the front room with George all of the sudden George walked to the recliner chair Sarah was sitting in her dad bent over in front of Sarah and began to squeeze Sarah arm real tight.

"Dad what the hell is wrong with you?", Sarah shouted. He gave her a death stare, and George then shot off running to the door trying to get out of the house, but the door was locked. George stood there yanking on the door. "Daddy what's wrong! Are you okay?" Sarah screamed. She went to grab the phone to call the police. George snapped out of it walked to the couch sat down and started laughing at the television as if nothing had just happened. Sarah stood there staring at her father in shock, scared in disbelief." Okay I think it's time to go, it's getting even more weird every day.

I wonder if they are on any kind of drugs or something this is just not normal. Sarah said to herself, "What are you looking at Sarah are you okay? ", George asked Sarah. "Do you remember anything about what just happened dad? You really freaked me out!", Sarah yelled while shaking nervously. "I don't know what you are talking about, Sarah you tripping." He was clueless about what had just taken place not even five minutes ago. "This has to be some type of joke my dad is playing on me to make me leave or something," and that was one way to scare the life out of her and make Sarah hit the roads without any hesitation.

Sarah sat in the front room to observe her dad and await on Jane. Jane finally walked into the door. Sarah jumped up and rushed to meet Jane at the door. Sarah began to tell Jane what had happened while she was gone. Jane laughed loudly. Congratulations you have gotten your first chance to experience George having an episode". Sarah stood

there confused. "What do you mean episode? What is an

episode, Jane?", Sarah asked in an aggravated tone. "Calm

down Sarah, your dad has abnormal seizures. He usually

stares or takes off running when the seizure happens. "He fell

down several floors of a casino boat and landed at the bottom

of the deck. His brain is damaged and every time he drinks

with his medicine he seizes.", Jane explained as best she

coulld. "So, you're telling me that you gave my dad all of this

liquor and beer, knowing it causes seizures. ARE YOU

CRAZY?!", Sarah shouted at Jane.

"Look Sarah, your dad is grown he can handle

himself." Sarah walked to her room and slammed the door

behind her. She was livid. This woman was killing her dad

slowly. She asked Jane plenty of times not to give George

any liquor or at least slowly wean him off of it. Jane just

ignored her request and continued giving him the beer and

liquor. George was so used to having his drinks every day

and if he didn't everyone knew. Bags would form under his eyes and he would be weak the entire day. Sometimes he wouldn't not move from the couch.

Every time George had a seizure Jane would call the ambulance and refused to ride with him. "Oh, I'm not going to the hospital with him, he'll be okay. I will call every one and tell them where he is being treated.", Jane said those words every single time she called the ambulance. His alcohol intake increased day by day. He became emotional and verbal abusive to both Jane and Sarah. He began to call Sarah terrible names and was downright disrespectful to her. Oftentimes, Sarah overlooked the things he said and chalked it up to the excessive liquor speaking.

One day George struck a nerve. Sarah sat at the table and George started talking out his head as usual, with a beer in his hand. He looked at Sarah with his glossy red eyes and boldly said, "B****! you are not even my daughter, you are for that dead man." George was speaking of Sarah's stepfather whom her mother married. He was the father of her three older sisters.

Sarah's face turned red. She stood up and walked over to her dad, pointed her finger in his face, stared him dead in his drunken, red, glossy eyes; and yelled" HOW DARE YOU! Say those words to me! After all of the damage you've done to me. I have suffered many years because of how you abandoned me and my brothers. You did what you die because you wanted to lay up with trash and drink your life away. You refused to handle your responsibilities as a father! What did you do to my mother? Are you the reason she's sick? You beat her until she could take no more? Did you verbally abuse my mother? Did you do her, just like you are doing to me?" Sarah continued questioning him as the tears flowed down her face.

"You need help, you are a very sick man. Because of you my mother is barely living a normal life!", Sarah shouted. "Your mother went crazy on her own. She drank herself to the life she is living now. She wasn't an angel, she had her faults too. So, don't put it all on me. I was there for your sisters before I kids with your mother. She was an alcoholic just like me! I just finished what your stepdad started.", George responded, with a smirk on his face.

Sarah got sick to her stomach, ran to her room, and cried and sobbed for about an hour. She was in disbelief, the words her father spoke to her were harsh and hard to hear. Now, she would have to act like none of those events took plase. She was supposed to be heading to a wedding rehearsal. One of her nieces was getting married that night at 7 o'clock p.m.. She had to find a way to shake back. "You can take the truck if you need it.", George said while throwing the keys on the bed. Sarah thought maybe that was his way of trying to get back on good terms. He had never offered the truck before, she always had to ask him. However, she didn't engage in conversation with George, she got the keys off the bed, and headed to rehearsal.

When Sarah arrived back from wedding rehearsal, she opened the door with her house keys, and there were her belongings sitting in the doorway. Everything packed up along with her blankets. Sarah looked at George "So you putting me out in the cold with nowhere to go, in the middle of the night?" YES! B****! My girlfriend wants you out of here. And I told you, you're not my daughter. You are for that dead man!" Sarah didn't say a word. Sarah grabbed her things, headed out the door, and down the road to make a call. She needed a ride and now a safe place to go.

Chapter 7

Sarah's niece, Shayla picked her up but had nowhere or Sarah to sleep. "I'll just sleep in your car until I find someplace to go." "Okay! Sarah you know if I had my own place you wouldn't have to go through any of this." Shayla assured her. "Yea, I know.", Sarah said in a hopeless voice. One day while sitting in the car, it started raining really hard outside and inside of the car. Her niece's window didn't go all the way up, and she got soaked.

Suddenly she had a thought of a long-time friend named Rodney. They hadn't been in contact for years, but every time Sarah and Rodney spoke, it was as if they never lost connection. They would always pick back up where they left off. Sarah dialed Rodney's number, to her surprise, it worked! "Hey Rodney!" Sarah was so relieved when Rodney answered the phone. "Hey skweetie pie!" Rodney always mispronounced his words. He would say a word using the "K" sound, but the word never had a "K" in them.

Sarah would always burst out laughing at his pronunciation but not this time. "How have you been Stanka?" I'm good, how you been stanka?" Sarah and Rodney always had cute nicknames for each other. Well, I'm not really sure at the moment. My dad put me out and now I'm living in my niece's car. Sarah so embarrassed but felt comfortable venting to Rodney. When he heard what she said happened and where she was living, he quickly went to talk with his mom. "Mama my friend is sleeping in a car, she has nowhere to go, its cold and raining outside. Sarah could hear Rodney's mom clear as day, "Boy if you don't tell that girl get over here right now. There is no way an 18-year-old, young woman should be living like.

Sarah caught a ride to Rodney's house and his mother Ann agreed to let Sarah live with them, as long as Rodney would promise to stay focused in school. He was close to graduation and she wanted him to finish strong. Rodney and Sarah slept in the same room. She always made sure Rodney was up every morning for school. She was like his very own alarm clock. The majority of the time, while Rodney attended school, Sarah would isolate herself in his bedroom."Let me guess, you never left the room today?" "No, Sarah said softly. I'm shy around new people." My sisters and mom are really cool, they wouldn't harm you or make you feel uncomfortable in any way.", Rodney said. "I know, I have to get the feel of everyone first. Eventually, I'll ease up if they are as nice of people you claim them to be.", Sarah responded.

Sarah did get to know his sisters and mother. They were just as supportive as Bee and Ms.Pam. The month of May came quickly. Rodney kept his promise to his mom. He graduated from high school and everyone was so excited and happy for him. "YOU GO, BOY! You did it!" Sarah screamed for Rodney so much at the graduation, she was hoarse, and no longer had a voice. Shortly after Rodney's graduation, Sarah and Rodney became very close. They were more than just best friends now, they were soul mates.

A couple of months after his graduation, Sarah became pregnant with their first child. Sadly, the baby died due to spontaneous miscarriage. Sarah was severely depressed even though she tried not to focus too much on the loss. "I really wanted that baby; I always have the worst luck in my life Sarah.", She said while tears dropped from her already puffy eyes. "Bae, we are still young we have a lot of time to have children. Lets just focus on ourselves right now, what's meant to be will be.", Rodney said while cuddling Sarah and pulling her closer to him.

At a follow up exam after the miscarriage, Sarah's doctor told her that it would be small chance she would be able to get pregnant again. He said she had a tilted cervix and they saw abnormal cells in the results from her pap smear. Sarah called Rodney screaming and shouting into the phone,

"Omg bae, the doctors are saying I have abnormal cells and it could even be cervical cancer. I May not ever be able to have kids." Bae calm down and let them retest you. The pap smear result may correct itself over time." Rodney was always the calm one when it came to freak, crazy things like this. He was Sarah's peace. Sarah was glad to have someone there to reassure her when things got out of control. "Okay babe, I'm just freaking out! I love you and thank you for keeping me calm."

Three months down the line Sarah had to redo her pap smear, and she decided she wanted to get on birth control. "Sarah, I need you to urinate in the cup before I put you on birth control. I have to be sure that you're not pregnant." She headed to the bathroom and gave the nurse a sample of urine. Sarah impatiently waited for the doctor to come back into the room. She was nervous and worried she would be pregnant because she and Rodney never used contraceptives. "Well you won't be getting any birth control today." Sarah did the face in palm." From the information that you've given, you should be about five weeks. It is very early.", the doctor said while smiling. "Congratulations Sarah!"

"We will call you next week with results from your second pap smear." "Okay thanks, doc!" Sarah rushed outside of the doctor's office and called Rodney. "I'm ready and pregnant.", she said quick. "Okay I'm on my way. Wait, what did you say Sarah?" "Please, don't be mad at me but I'm pregnant again.", she said nervously walking around the parking lot. "Why would I be mad? I'm not mad, I hope it's a boy." Sarah laughed and was relieved that he wasn't upset with her. When Rodney pulled up, Sarah jumped happily into the car. "We are about to go get some pregnancy tests. I want to see this for myself!" Rodney said excitedly and with a huge smile on his face. "Ok let's go get some and I'll use the bathroom in front of you since you're a skeptic." Sarah and Rodney laughed out loud.

They made it home, and Sarah rushed to take the at-home pregnancy test. Immediatelty, two lines appeared. Sarah smiled big and handed the test to Rodney. "See I told you so, we are having a baby." They both stood there staring at the test for what seemed like five minutes." Come on we have to go tell my mama.", Rodney said and then grabbed her hand. Sarah and Rodney walked into Ms. Ann's house. "Mama! We have to tell you something."

"What is it, Rodney?" "We are having a baby!" "Stop playing with me Rodney, where is the test?" Sarah nervously handed her the test. "Girrrrrl, I hope you give me my first granddaughter!" Sarah smiled and hugged her. Rodney's family was so excited for them.

In preparation or the baby, they decided to cover all of their basis. They both had steady jobs. Sarah's foster mother let them rent out her one-bedroom rent house. They were on their own, in a house, and they loved it. They soon found out they were having a baby boy. They all did a lot of shopping for the new baby.

Rodney Jr was well prepared for his entrance into this world. Sarah carried Rodney Jr up until 39 weeks and 1 day. Sarah was medically induced because the baby was causing a lot of medical problems for Sarah. Sarah was admitted to the hospital where they started her on Pitocin.An hour later Sarah started feeling contractions, but with each contraction that came Rodney Jr heart rate began to drop." Code blue!!!! Code BLUE the doctors screamed.

Sarah and Rodney became worried. The doctors rushed into the room and put an oxygen mask on Sarah's face." your son heart right is just dropping we have to get him out now we are going to perform a C-Section! Sarah began to cry and break down. "Stop crying I am going to be with you and nothing is going to go wrong.

Our son will be here in no time .I'm going to hold your hand the whole time bae I promise ." you are always so reassuring bae thank you so much. Rodney prepped in all blue hospital wear. Sarah was rolled to the emergency operating room where she received her epidural. Rodney walked into the room and stood where Sarah was lying in bed. Sarah body was so numb up she couldn't feel a thing.

"Bae can you feel that? your stomach is wide open. Rodney began to squeal and gag. your guts are out bae! Sarah laid on the surgery table laughing at laughing at Rodney saying well I bet you won't get me pregnant again." Sarah and Rodney laughed. Sarah gave birth to a healthy six-pound Rodney Jr. she couldn't believe she just gave birth via c-section to a baby the doctors said she wouldn't be able to carry. Her miracle baby had finally arrived.

Rodney returned to work shortly after Sarah, and their baby boy returned home. She took her six-week maternity leave to care for the baby and heal.Everything was so perfect for Sarah." I can't believe I went from being homeless to having my own family "Sarah thought to herself while staring at her baby boy in her arms. " Mommy loves you Rodney Jr. Sarah went from having nothing to being in the nail shop every Friday, having nice clothes, The best of shoes and the well-done hairstyles. Sarah and the baby never went out because Rodney Sr made sure they had everything.

Rodney even brought Sarah an Infiniti J30; her car had all brown leather on the side with seat warmers. Sarah felt good having all these material things, but something was still missing. Sarah and Rodney began to disagree on a lot of things. Their life became strictly about their son, The laughs and jokes came to an end. They had more laughs time for friends than their relationship itself.Eventually, Sarah and Rodney began to fuss every night.

They decided to take a break. "I need to get away can the baby, and I come stay with you for a couple of days? Sarah had called Bee." why are you even asking that you know you 'all are welcome over here at any time, besides my daughter needs a playmate" Bee had just given birth to her

firstborn daughter five months before Sarah had her son.
Sarah headed to bee house and took the baby with her. Sarah
laid the baby down so she can take a breather and vent to
Bee. "Girl lately I have just been so frustrated. I don't know,
but maybe we have to just get used to being young parents.
"Yea that's probably what it is, my daughter's dad and me
been cranky a lot too. "Hold up bee let me take this call
"hello "where you at?

My best friend and I just got into a fight, and he pulled a
gun out on me "What? I'm on my way !!Sarah and bee
buckled the kids in her car and headed to where Rodney was.
"Sarah jumped out the car leaving one slipper behind.
Rodney and his friend were in the middle of the street
fighting Sarah went to hit Rodney friend until they all burst
out laughing." It's a joke Sarah calm down. "Sarah's face
turned red "Do you think this is funny? I ran red lights and
was doing 80 over here with kids in the car." and you all
think this is funny? "Sarah jumped in her car and sped off.

She was embarrassed and pissed that Rodney would

play a stupid prank on her at such a crucial time in her life.

Sarah told Rodney she couldn't do it anymore she needs time

to figure out if this is what she wanted. little did she know

this break would end her relationship with her soul mate

forever. Rodney moved on only two weeks later. He had

found him a new friend that eventually turned into a

girlfriend. Sarah couldn't believe her world came crashing

down on her that fast and the love her life was now loving

another woman.

    " Well, I guess if it's that easy to move on he never

really loved me as he said, you just don't be with a person for

two and a half years and best friends of five years and move

on with your life like that. Sarah cried on Bee's shoulder.

Everything was now gone from Sarah within a blink of an

eye. Why? how? how could this be I had everything in my

hands now it's gone. I let everything go over a stupid prank.

Sarah was very disappointed with herself that she didn't fight for her relationship. Sarah went from 145 pounds to 97 pounds.

Sarah didn't eat or sleep anymore, and she struggled with having the energy to take care of her child. She was too depressed to do anything in life. Although Rodney walked out of her life, Bee stayed in her corner, and helped Sarah out with her son on the days he wouldn't be with his dad." Girl, you would not believe all the presents mama got our kids for Christmas." I can only imagine she spoiled us rotten, so I can only imagine what she is about to do for our kids."

Thank you for everything BEE.I really appreciate it." Girl please you know we do you will always be family to us." Yeah, I know, but I really need to get it together Bee ...If I lose any more weight, everybody will think I have some type of sickness. Sarah and bee chuckled while hugging each other.Tears began to flow down Sarah's cheeks "It hurt so bad Bee sometimes I feel like I'm dying inside. I just wish it was easy for me like it was easy for him." You will get there baby girl it won't happen overnight, but one day you will get that smile back."

I hope so because this is for the birdman." Bee and Sarah sat outside talking and crying the whole night. Whiles. Pam kept the kids company. Sarah lived with Bee and Ms.Pam for over a little over a year.Bee and Sarah raised their kids together.Sarah did some soul searching and devoting her time to working and caring for her son while co-parenting with Rodney.

After going through the heartaches of her broken relationship, Sarah finally came to the conclusion that it was never really her fault that her relationship with Rodney failed and it wasn't over a silly joke it was way deeper than what she never took the time to comprehend. Sarah break up was destined to be.Rodney was the best father to their son, He was a good boyfriend some days ...but Rodney lacked empathy in any many places.Sarah always sensed that Rodney considered those material things would count as being a perfect boyfriend, but Sarah longed for much more than material things. Yes it was nice Sarah had her nails done, hair fixed, and shoes and clothing but whatsoever happened to loving her? Sarah and Rodney had two different up bringing's. Rodney was raised with going to school with the trending Jordan shoes and name brand clothing. Sarah went to school with a pair of light up sketchers. Her shoes and clothing weren't very trendy, but it meant the world to her because she was grateful even to have a pair of shoes.

Sarah wanted Rodney to see that even with all the finest material things people can still feel less fortunate and unloved. Material things never meant much to Sarah if she had it she had it if she did not then that's what it was. If you don't have these nice things that doesn't mean you're beneath the next person. Sometimes Sarah felt Rodney looked at her like the scum of the earth because she wasn't on his level material wise. Sarah importance was the craving for consistency of love and affection.

The sensitivity Sarah was feeling from her and Rodney relationship traced back to searching for love and acceptance in all the wrong places. Sarah father rejected her from his love, so Sarah looked for affection elsewhere in men. Rodney tried to repair Sarah and show Sarah a different lifestyle that was appealing but lacked love and affection.

Chapter 8

Two years later Rodney and Sarah were co-parenting well.
They became great at it over the years. Sarah ultimately grew
to love and accept Rodney significant other.If Sarah had to
hand pick her, herself she would. She loved their child as if
he was her very own. She was the stepmother any one child
could ask for. She had been in Rodney Jr life since the age of
five months old.

With time Sarah moved on with her life and was now in
a new relationship. A friend of Sarah introduced her to this
man name Kenneth. Kenneth was very sweet but way much
older than Sarah. Kenneth rubbed Sarah back after long days
of work, their dates were simple, like walks on the levee.
Kenneth worked on Sarah car and even did light housework
on Sarah house. Sarah had a night time job as a caregiver, her
own house, and her own transportation.

Kenneth had a part-time job. Sarah fell in love with Kenneth because he seemed to be very humble and understanding. Little did Sarah know that she was on a hell for a ride of her life. Everything was thought to be good to Sarah. Sarah had accomplished a lot within the past two years, and she was finally on her feet in a good space. Kenneth and Sarah would have small arguments here and there. Sarah and Kenneth would get on the game and play zombies call of duty to relieve their stress, and by the end of the game, they were making love to each other. Six months into the relationship Sarah ended up pregnant with Kenneth child.

Sarah called Kenneth after leaving the doctor "I am pregnant ."You gone kill it right ?"Sarah and Kenneth had talked about abortion in the past, but Sarah didn't assume for those to be Kenneth first words ."I'm not killing my baby Kenneth ...either you are going to be there are you're not it's your choice , Sarah shouted while hanging the phone up in

Kenneth's face ."I can't believe this man just flat out asked me if I was going to kill our own child. I can never bring myself to doing something like that without that being on my heart .it will eat me alive". Sarah thought to herself. Kenneth choice was to run away from his responsibility.Kenneth proceeded to let the world know how he wants no part in the child Sarah was bringing into the world, He ranted on social media and blasted Sarah and her unborn "I don't want Sarah baby, F*** her and that baby she did it on purpose, she knew I didn't want kids for her ".

A friend saw the post and called Sarah." girl did you see what Kenneth just posted on Facebook?" No, I'm about to go see. Sarah was livid; she was on furious. She immediately called Kenneth. He sent her to the voicemail, Sarah talked on the voicemail as if it were him on the phone "You are a sorry piece of man how are you going to get mad at me because I don't want to kill my child !!!Your child!!!!! This is our baby we are talking about. your blood is running through this child, you are the most evil man I ever met, but you don't have to worry about us we are going to be fine with or without you.

" Sarah shouted at the voicemail and hung up the phone crying in disbelief. "What am I going to do now? I can't raise a child by myself." Sarah grew angry with herself every day." How could I be so stupid and lay down with a dog and get up with fleas? How could I put my child through the same exact thing my father put me through. I don't want my baby going through the same heartaches I had.My baby might not be as strong as me when it grows older.

Sarah was ashamed and disappointed with herself. Her heart was aching for her future child. Sarah was fine being single, but she didn't want her mistake to inflict upon her child life ...Sarah went to all of her prenatal care visits alone. Sarah cried every single night. "How could I be so naive. I should have known better Sarah cried while holding her stomach.

Sarah saw several red flags, but she disregarded them all. All the women in Kenneth inbox that he denied to her in front of her face. Sarah never saw Kenneth with his other children. Kenneth wasn't raised by his mother nor father, so Kenneth never knew how to love someone genuinely. Sarah should have been aware, but she was too stupid looking for love once again in a man. Sarah went on to find out she was having another baby boy. Sarah hadn't talked to Kenneth in a while Sarah had lost her house and her job and became homeless again. Sarah then moved to a shelter an hour and a half away from her hometown because she knew her family was not going to let her return. Every time Sarah would become homeless majority of the times she had to live in shelters because no one was willing to accept her and her son without giving them a move out date or without Sarah overhearing family members discussing her and her child being annoying. Sarah grew bitter because she watched the doors open and plenty of chances being given to her nieces and nephews but the minute Sarah asked for help it was either no or she was being talked about. The most heart-wrenching situation for Sarah was that her siblings would never let theirchildren go to a shelter, but it was fine with everyone being content while Sarah and her children were in shelters. Sarah never felt pleasing to her family and neither worthy. Sarah started traveling unfamiliar roads and cities and to complete strangers for help. What bothered Sarah so much was the favoritism that was being shown between sisters and their children. Sarah nieces and nephews had never been homeless a day in their life as many times as they have made mistakes in life, Sarah siblings would open the doors for their children but Sarah just wasn't good enough or either she couldn't stay long enough until she was well established again. One day Sarah received a local phone call from prison." Hey, Sarah, it's me, Kenneth, answer the phone. Sarah accepted the phone call." hey I'm in jail this call is only for two minutes but I'm calling you to check on the baby.

" The baby is fine, I'm having a boy." are you going to give him my middle name?" I'll think about it." The phone hung up. Sarah rolled her eyes while hanging up the phone," He must be out of his mind. My child will never have anything of him. Kenneth went as far spending his last checks before he went to jail, putting money on the phone so he can call Sarah every no

The months leading up to the end of her pregnancy Sarah decided to give in and ask her sister Shanice can she come live with her, until she got her on her feet. Her sister told her yes. Sarah was nearing the end of her pregnancy. Sarah was at her sister's house relaxing when she got an inbox on Facebook." Girrrrrl your baby daddy out of jail huh?" Wait, what? How do you know that? He never got in touch with me and told me he was out of jail!

Sarah was very angry "how in the hell I'm three weeks away from giving birth to your child, and you don't even reach out to me, but you made sure you kept in contact with me when you was in jail?" Sarah pressure felt like it went straight through the roof "this dude have him some nerves, but I'm going to show him better than I can tell him. Sarah blocked Kenneth off of all social networks and changed her number. The next day Sarah went to Bee's house to let some steam off and vent eat some seafood." I heard if you drink pineapple juice and eat seafood with a teaspoon of castor oil it makes you go into labor. "Bee said with a smirk on her face. Sarah laughed

." Well, there is only one way to find out, right? Sarah said while laughing. Sarah finished her seafood, pineapple juice and had a teaspoon of castor oil, Sarah began to gag, ahhhh!" Man, that's some nasty stuff, Bee. I hope it works because I will not drink another spoon of it.! Bee laughed." let's get home just in case labor starts for you. Sarah, Bee, and

Bee sister headed to the house. When they arrived at Ms.Pam

house, Sarah started having contractions.

''Whoa that was a painful one.'' oh my GOD you had a

contraction, Sarah, it's working! "Bee began shouting. Sarah

rushed to the bathroom as she felt a lot of pressure. BEEEEE!

Sarah screamed from the bathroom." what!!! What!!?? Did

your water break? NO! But it's time get the car ready!!!Bee

and her sister quickly grabbed Rodney Jr, and they headed to

drop him off to Rodney Sr." Don't you have this baby in this

car! Keep those legs together we are almost there. Bee sister

was running red lights and was driving what felt like 100

mph, on airline highway.

They finally arrived at the hospital." Okay, sissy let's get

you checked in. Bee answered all questions for Sarah while

being admitted to labour and delivery. Sarah rocked back and

forth as Bee comforted her. Sarah was admitted to the

hospital in active labour." Ma'am, you are steadily asking me

all these questions!!!just give me my epidural NOW!!!!!!

Sarah screamed in agony through every contraction until her medicine kicked in. Sarah received her epidural, and everything was smooth sailing.

Bee was drained from all the labor coaching; she slept majority of the time.." Bee, it's time to get up.! the baby is coming. Bee jumped up "okay sissy let's do this you can do it! Sarah gave three pushes and out came her five-pound baby boy. She called him Noel. Bee was the very first person to see and hold Noel. She walked over with Noel "look sissy he looks just like his dad Kenneth." oh my GOD he does look like him, but he is a way handsome version, Sarah laughed and smiled as Bee reached her Noel." hey handsome you finally made it huh.

Your big brother Rodney can't wait to meet you." I'm going to get some rest at home, sis call me if you need me okay" Bee walked out the room with drowsy eyes." love you, sis, thanks for the support." Sarah put Rodney in his bassinet and fell sound asleep. Sarah was discharged two days later. Sarah was raising her baby boy on her own.

Rodney Jr bonded with baby Noel very well, but some days he would be flat out frustrated" Mommy cut that light off and feed your baby or something, he isn't nothing but a crybaby. "Sarah laughed and cut the light off, and rocked baby Noel back to sleep. Life wasn't that bad for Sarah raising her new son alone. During the first couple of months in Noel life, his dad was back in jail. Once again Kenneth blew up Sarah phone." You have a collect call from "Kenneth."

OH gosh not again !!!Sarah accepted the call. "So what are you in jail for now "I got into some confusion with my baby mama but how are you and my son?" we are fine, we are living ."So I've been thinking and it came to mind that you are the only one that is there for me when I need you , I love you, and I want to be in my son life , when I am released from jail I want to marry you Sarah ...we always let other people tear us apart and I'm going to change for you, I'm going to be proactive in my son life ".Kenneth sounded very convincing to Sarah. Sarah's naïve thinking and tender heart fell for Kenneth promises.

She always believed in giving more chances than one deserved. "Okay, Kenneth so how long do you have in jail? Well, I'm only sitting on traffic charges right now maybe you can call around and make some calls to see if they can release me early due to the charges being so old, you know when it comes to stuff like this you are book smart you just aren't street sense." Sarah laughed. Yes, Kenneth call me tomorrow I'll see what I can do.

" The next day bright and early Sarah made several calls over the next few days Sarah finally got in touch with the right person. Sarah talked with the mayor of the city where Kenneth was stationed at. After doing a lot of convincing and promising the mayor, Kenneth would keep up with his court date they released Kenneth on parole.Sarah was so excited, and impatiently awaited on Kenneth phone call "Kenneth

pack your stuff you are about to get out!" I did it, Kenneth!

You are about to be released!

Stop playing are you serious? Sarah, I wouldn't lie to you

Kenneth I'm serious.!! Sarah shouted!!" baby they just called

my name I will call you when I'm out, my first stop will be

you!" Okay, I'm going to be waiting for you. One hour later

Kenneth was knocking on Sarah door. Sarah threw on some

lipstick and brushed her hair quickly and ran to open the

door. Sarah jumped in Kenneth's arms wrapping her legs and

arms around him "you must have missed me huh "Kenneth

said with a smile

. Yes, I did Sarah said while kissing him on the lips. Here

is Baby Noel. Sarah said while handing Noel over to

Kenneth. Sarah and Kenneth made love late that night,

showered and went straight to bed cuddling their son Noel.

Sarah was working at Popeye's at the time And had been in

her studio apartment for 6 months alone with her kids. Sarah made friend with her next-door neighbor, Sarah neighbor got

her own at Popeye's. Sarah neighbor name was Shaniqua.

Shaniqua aunt offered to keep Sarah kids while she worked

for her mother at Popeye's and Shaniqua sister would pick

Sarah up every morning for work. Sarah took the offer her

neighbor presented to her.

Sarah went to work every day but Sunday's. Shaniqua

and Sarah became close anytime Sarah needed anything

Shaniqua could depend on her. Kenneth got on at that plant

making good money, and Sarah was in the middle of

transferring jobs. Sarah started working at a dollar general up

the street from the house. Sarah paid for all of Kenneth tools

for work. Things were on the upside at home. Everything

decided to fall into place until Sarah lost her job at dollar

general.

Sarah had got hired at UPS temporarily making ten dollars

an hour. Sarah came home from a long day at work and there

stood Kenneth in the front room "So you think you are

somebody just because you work at UPS?" that's nothing compared to somebody who makes fifteen dollars an hour, and after the holiday they are going to fire you, you do know that right ? Kenneth started laughing then proceeded to get in bed "."Why do you have to belittle me, Kenneth?".

I'm just telling you like it is, so you won't get your hopes up high." Sarah ignored him, took a shower and went to bed. Kenneth wouldn't even bring Sarah back and forth to and from work even when he had   his own transportation." Call your friend and tell her to bring you, since she is always doing stuff for you, you aren't anything but a charity case anyway." Kenneth started laughing and walked out the door. The verbal abuse became the new normal for him. every single day Kenneth had nothing pleasing to say about Sarah. Eventually, the emotional abuse took a toll on Sarah mental health.

After Sarah got laid off from U.P.S, Kenneth took that to his advantage to mind control Sarah even more so Kenneth made Sarah feel like the scum of the earth. He paid bills and threw it back in her face. One day Kenneth and Sarah got into a heated argument, and Sarah couldn't take it anymore. You're nothing but a big f*** up that's why your family don't love you , one of your family members even tried having sex with me, but I turned them down on the strength of you "Kenneth shouted!

" bring me to my sister house Kenneth I don't even want to stay here anymore. "I'll give this apartment up just to get away from you". Tears streamed down Sarah's face., while packing her, Noel and Rodney Jr belongings. Kenneth agreed to bring Sarah to her sister house." Kayla, I can't do it anymore, Kenneth is mentally abusing me, he pays the rent, but I can't be with him anymore. "Sarah calm down, you know you can come live here go get the rest of your things.

" Sarah dried her eyes and returned home with Kenneth to grab more things. Sarah got a text message from Kayla that read "I'm sorry baby sis, I didn't tell my husband you were coming so he said no that you can't come ."Sarah didn't reply back she told Kenneth never mind about her moving,"I told your dumb a** your family doesn't care about you, I just wanted you to see that for yourself.

I'm the only one loves you. Kenneth had a smirk on his face. Sarah couldn't say anything but," yeah, maybe you're right." Sarah got into bed and cried, Kenneth turned his back to her and went straight to bed. Sarah felt trapped in a relationship she desperately wanted to get out. Sarah had no way out. 'This is what I get for chasing after a man who doesn't want me. I deserve this; I always give people more chances than they deserve and I repeatedly get hurt in the end. Sarah was destroyed and broken.

"Kenneth paid all the bills there was no way Sarah could leave. He had Sarah just where he wanted her. Sarah looked at herself in the bathroom mirror and began to cry out to GOD. "What are you trying to do to me? I'm broken already, why don't you just get me out of this situation." Sarah felt betrayed by GOD even though she chooses to make her own careless decisions, but she desperately cried for GOD to help her out that abusive relationship.

Chapter 9

Sarah's heart was broken. She blamed GOD for the mess continuously." Why are you allowing me to be broken over and over again? "Sarah cried her heart out to GOD. **Sometimes we blame GOD when we are going through situations, and he will let us return to that situation over and over again until we refuse to turn to that situation.** And that's exactly where Sarah was at in her life. Sarah kept trying to repair a broken situation that was not meant to be repaired. A week later Sarah had a mental break down, and she found herself back in the mental institution for severe depression. After Sarah was released, she went to live with her sister Shanice, because Kenneth no longer wanted to pay the bills anymore." I hope you figure out what you going to do about your living situation because I am not paying your bills anymore, go ask the people who so-called care about you.

" Are you serious Kenneth when you didn't have a job I worked every day to pay the bills, and you are going to let your son, and I become homeless because you decide you don't want to pay any bills?" Sarah left her apartment behind. Sarah first day home she had found out Kenneth had moved into her apartment and had his new girlfriend spending nights.

Kenneth kept telling Sarah he was out of town at a job but Sarah knew something was pretty off, and she was going to find out what it was very soon ." hay Kenneth where are you? is sick with a fever he needs to go to the doctor "Sarah had the phone glued to her ear while trying to listen to anything suspicious in Kenneth background. "I'm out of town in New Orleans; I can't."

Sarah knew Kenneth wasn't telling the truth, so she caught a ride to her old apartment to see if his car was parked at the apartment. Sure enough, it was. Sarah dialed Kenneth number." how are you out of town, but your car is parked at the apartment.?" Okay, I lied I talked to your landlord when you left, and I convinced him to let me live in the apartment since you couldn't afford it anymore and I could since I am the breadwinner.

"So you went behind my back, and you moved into the apartment, I had to beg you to pay the bills where you laid your head at ? also, you refused to keep a roof over your son's head ."Look you said you weren't staying there because you didn't have the money and as long as you were there I wasn't paying any more bills so go ask your family and friends. "Kenneth hung the phone up in Sarah's face and had her phone turned off, so she wouldn't be able to call him back.

The apartment Sarah worked so hard to get while Kenneth was in prison was now occupied by him and new fling, But even that wasn't enough for Sarah not to return back to Kenneth, the man that treated her like complete scum. Sarah was weak for Kenneth and no matter how bad he treated her all she wanted was someone to accept her because her whole life was full of rejection

She was so desperate that she would do anything for a man to accept her and child. A few months down the line Sarah moved in with her sister Marie so she could find job placement and a babysitter for her kids. Hoping that she would be able to get back on her feet and possibly get her a home. That didn't last long for Sarah at all." Hey Sarah, my landlord, saw you at over here and you're not on the lease, so you are going to have to go, Marie told Sarah.

" Okay that's fine I don't want to get you put out your home I'll just go to Alabama and see if they would have some shelters me and my kids could go to, I'll be gone by tomorrow when you get off. Rodney was never too fund of his son going to a shelter, but Sarah always reassured him she would take care of their son. Sarah called her brother Patrick wife to take them to Alabama.

" Hey Shayla, can you bring the boys and me to Alabama because we have to leave Marie house because her landlord found out we are staying here. Sarah began to cry on the phone. She was so tired of moving around with her babies. She started to feel like she was a failure at being a mother because she could never keep a stable place her kids could call home.

" Don't cry Sarah maybe you need a change, maybe you need to get away, so you can get yourself together, do you know anybody in Alabama?". Yes, I know one girl I was friends with in the past she said we could come stay until I find a good shelter.". "Okay, pack your things I'll be on my way in the morning. Sarah packed her things, and Shayla and Sarah hit the road with her kids the next morning.

Sarah held her tears the whole time. She had to be strong for her babies." Sarah arrived at her friend house and stayed there for a week. She was very homesick, but she knew she couldn't return back to her hometown because she had nowhere to return to. The following week Sarah got accepted into a women's shelter.

" Okay boys we are going to a summer camp for the summer, and we are going to have lots of fun, but there are going to be rules at the summer camp that you and mommy have to follow. Whatever the teachers tell us to do we have to do okay?".

Sarah couldn't bring herself to tell her babies they were really in a shelter. It broke her heart she had to lie them but explaining where they really would have caused her to much pain. Sarah and the boys shared one room together, but they each had their own beds.There rooms resembled something like a hotel. Sarah and the boys also had their own bathroom which was perfect because they didn't need a reason to come out the room besides to eat.

Sarah wanted to avoid all the other ladies in the shelter. She isolated herself from everyone. Sarah had no words to say; her heart was so heavy. Some days Sarah would bring the

113

boys out the room, and other days she just wasn't up for it.

She kept in contact with her friend. "Hay do you want to go

to six flags this weekend with my family." Sure, I'll call

Rodney Jr dad and tell him to wire some money down here.

The boys will most definitely love that.

  Rodney Sr wired the money so Sarah and the kids can go

to six flags in Atlanta. The boys and Sarah enjoyed

themselves they rode many rides and even got in a wave

pool. Sarah needed that break. They stayed in Atlanta for the

full weekend. and Returned to Alabama for that Monday.

Sarah had to be back at the shelter shortly because they only

gave her a two-day pass.

  " Well back to the hell hole we go." Sarah rolled her

eyes while buzzing the door to be opened. "Come on boys we

are back at summer camp." aww mommy we want to go back

to six flags we tired of being here. Rodney Jr begins to whine

while tugging at Sarah's arm."I'm sorry baby, but we will go

back next year sometime it's time to go to summer camp now

."Sarah and the boys headed to their room, showered and went to bed from having a long exhausted day. The next couple of days the boys became very irritated from staying in the shelter. Over three days Sarah received three write-ups from the boys getting into fights with other kids and terrorizing the shelter.

The coordinator called Sarah into a meeting on a Sunday morning. "Sarah, we are sorry, but we are going to have to request you and your kids to leave the facility because we are getting too many complaints from other mothers concerning your children's behavior. "Ma'am we have nowhere to go, our hometown is three hours away, what are we supposed to do?" I'm sorry, but by tonight you will have to be gone, we wish you well Sarah".

" Sarah grabbed her boys and began to cry. "what's wrong mommy? We have to leave summer camp because my brother and I are bad.? "Sarah gazed into Rodney Jr eyes with tears coming down her face ."No baby it's okay, mommy had no business bring you all here from the beginning, but don't worry about that, mommy will find a place for us to go. Sarah kissed her boys, and they headed to pack their things.

Sarah knew that her boys wouldn't adjust to being at a shelter for long. They didn't know anyone there. They was forced to eat slop food and wasn't allowed to play at certain times. Sarah had to make a decision and make one fast or else they would have been on the streets. "The only person that would take me back is my Noel dad."

"Kenneth had been reaching out to Sarah for the past couple of weeks to get her to come back home and live with him in his new house ,but Sarah always rejected, and Said no because she knew Kenneth was still having relations with his new girlfriend but he told Sarah repeatedly that they were over, but Sarah knew for a fact they were far from over.Sarah had to suck it up bite the bullet and call Kenneth or else they would be stranded in a state they knew nothing about .

" Hey, do you still have your house?" Yes, are you coming down? I will be there late tonight we got put out the shelter, "Ok call me when you are here". Sarah hung up the phone and took a deep breath. Sarah got in touch with Shayla to come bring them home. When Sarah arrived at Kenneth house, he came and helped her unload her bags out the car. Sarah went and laid the boys down for bed.

Sarah and Kenneth got in bed and fell straight to sleep. He had to be at work the next morning, and she was exhausted from the three-hour ride. The next day Sarah and Kenneth had a long talk about his previous relationship." I'm really not with her she doesn't want me anymore because she thinks I'm still in love with you. "Are you? Sarah said, while side-eyeing Kenneth. This Sarah was not easily lured in by his many broken promises. Sarah had decided in her mind that living with Kenneth would be temporary until she was able to get on her feet until she found a stable place for her and the boys to live but for now, this was her only option. This time

Sarah stayed focus "Yes, I am Sarah, but you really get on my nerves sometimes.

You always listening to other people when it comes to our relationship. "Okay, I'm not going there with you tonight because we all know how you play your little games, Kenneth". Sarah went to go to bed, and Kenneth followed her. Kenneth fell asleep before Sarah. Sarah laid in bed replaying their recent conversation, and she knew something was very off, and she had to find out what it was, she knew him, and his fling were still having dealings with each other, but she had to find proof." search through his phone and see what's in there."

" Sarah quickly acted on her thoughts. Sarah took Kenneth phone off the charger and browsed through it She knew it was not right to be snooping, but she was anxious." I love you, me and Sarah not together I'm just helping her out because she had nowhere to go I don't even want her here.

Sarah's face turned red. Kenneth was once lying again to this female and to her. Just a couple hours ago he was telling Sarah how he wanted to be with her and he got the house just for them, but his text messages showed otherwise." I have never met a man who is such a compulsive liar, and so manipulative". Sarah wasn't even surprised about what she had just read because she knew that man wasn't going to change for anybody.

Sarah jumped into bed and started scrolling through her social network messages. She had received a message from one her ex-boyfriends from years ago." hey what's up, how have you been? Sarah hesitated to reply but thought it wouldn't hurt to reply, hell he entertaining his ex why can't I?"Hey, I'm okay what are you doing? Sarah was sure Kenneth was worn out in a deep sleep from a long day of work, but she was wrong.

He laid there reading every incoming message and outgoing message. Kenneth jumped up and snatched Sarah phone." You talking to other dudes while lying beside me huh B****?". I'm sorry I thought you were sleep and it was a harmless conversation like you were having with your ex right?

Kenneth walked to the bathroom filled up a sink of water and threw Sarah phone in it." What the hell are you doing!?Sarah screamed you are going to replace my phone! Kenneth took the phone and threw it against the wall. Sarah walked out the room and went into the kitchen. Kenneth came behind her and began to tussle with Sarah. He dragged her to the front room and put her on the couch.

Kenneth went to grab a bleach bottle and began to spray Sarah down from head to toe with bleach and grabbed a lighter and tried setting her own fire. "Get off my couch B**** I don't want you to set my furniture on fire while I light your a** up. Sarah began to scream "STOP!!!PLEASE!! My kids are in the next room. Sarah cried and screamed for her kids to wake up.Sarah figured if the boys came out the room he would stop. Sarah's kids came running out the room and stood in the doorway "Go back in your room. !!!Kenneth screamed at the kids. He finally let her up. Sarah went to comfort her kids in the bedroom. She held them and cried herself to sleep with her boys in her arms.

That was Kenneth first time physically abusing Sarah but it wasn't his last time. During a heated argument, Kenneth knocked Sarah unconscious in front of their son. Leaving her to wake up with her son standing over her screeching "Mommy !!Mommy wake- up "!!

By the time Sarah had awaken Kenneth was gone, and he took her phone with him. From that day forward Sarah has been free from Kenneth for two years now. Sarah knew it was no returning from that situation even if she wanted to. She knew she couldn't come back from that. Sarah would have lost her life that night. Kenneth didn't know if she was dead or alive. He left her laying on the kitchen floor and their child unattended while she laid there unconscious from being punched in the head.

Sarah maintained her distance from Kenneth and any time he wanted to see his son, it had to be done through a third party. Either She was going to make the decision that this man was going to cost her, her sanity or life or she was going to move on and leave the false dreams, abuse, hurt, and pain behind her! Sarah chooses her life and her kids, and this time she meant it.

Chapter 10

For the last couple of years, Sarah had spent her life mending relationships with her family, and old friends. Sarah and her kids have been living in their own home for one year now. She got back in touch with her dad and got to know more uncles and aunts on her dad side. Sarah sees her mom on occasions but is working on their bond.

She is stable in her life and now working two jobs to provide for her and her kids. She takes pride in knowing that no matter who rejects her she has a GOD who will never forsake her nor her kids. Sarah spent most of her time caring for her aunt who had cancer and providing for her boys. Sarah Aunt became a huge inspiration in her life.

Sarah got her courage from her aunt. She battled cancer and the torture of chemotherapy every week, but her aunt still woke up with a smile and praised GOD every day for a new day to be healed. "Neicey, I love you, and I want you to know it's never goodbye its see you later, "Sarah aunt told her those words every night.

Sarah believed if her aunt could do it so can she. Sarah lived every day with hope and joy being grateful the Lord woke her up to fight through another day. She grew to love and live life as it was presented to her. As time went on Sarah began to embrace her struggles because the pain was preparation for her destination. She was Strong and ready to take on the world.

Sarah had a few depressing days on the journey of healing after so much damage had been done, but the good had always outweighed the bad. Sarah began to visit old friends and her family including her dad. One-night Sarah was out at her friend house doing laundry, and she received a message from Marie, her sister. "Go check on dad NOW! Jane called and said he just had a heart attack.

"Sarah put her shoes on grabbed Noel and was headed out the door. Sarah phone starts to ring. It was her aunt, her dad sister "Niece!!!!George is dead!!!He is gone. Sarah aunt

screamed very loud !!Sarah dropped her phone and sped into

her car to head to George house.When she arrived, the police,

ambulance, and coroner was already stationed at her dads

house. Sarah reached her son to a family member and slowly

walked inside of her dad house.

There laid her father stretched out on the floor, dead from a

heart attack. Sarah fell to her knees unto her daddy's chest

and cried "Daddy I'm so sorry I said I was coming why didn't

you wait on me one more time. Please don't leave me, don't

do this to me. I never got the chance to tell you I forgive you.

I'm not mad at you anymore. Please don't leave, I'm sorry.

Sarah laid on her dad's chest and stroked his hair .it almost

felt like the tears were never-ending. Sarah was just getting to

a place where she accepted the pain her father inflicted unto

her, but she never got a chance to say those words to him.

She should have forgiven her dad a long time ago. After all

her dad put her through even after death, the pain of losing her dad took a piece of her soul.

Very seldom in life we hold back our love for our loved ones. We hold grudges against the people we love instead of forgiving them right away, maybe Sarah dad did not deserve flowers every day on earth, but her dad did deserved forgiveness **Matthew 6:15**. Sarah did things on her own time. She harbored all that hate and resentment in her heart for years. Now she was left to stand over father body and tell him she forgives him, but it was too late.

Sarah grieved very deeply. She had a little peace in knowing that her dad was free from all sickness and pain. But it hurt her heart seeing her dad leave so unexpectedly. Five days later Sarah lost her aunt to cancer. She had experienced two losses back to back. "Sarah cried curled up in her bed "but aunt tee you told me never say goodbye. So why would you leave me "? Sarah was being broken over and over, but this was a different kind of suffering. A pain she never knew she could ever feel. Every memory from her aunt and dad and all the good conversations and jokes they shared replayed in her mind.

She never experienced so much death of loved ones in such a short amount of time. But one thing Sarah knew for sure was her aunt was with the lord. She went on to accept the death of her loved ones, but she kept their memories alive. She became stronger each day. All the pain and suffering were now over with. Throughout everything Sarah experienced. The heartaches, depression, suicidal attempts, low self-esteem, mental abuse, physical abuse, and being a motherless and fatherless child and being rejected by so many family members, she had faith as small as a mustard seed **(Luke 17:6)**, and that's all Sarah needed to get through. She wasn't lost!.

Sarah had to go through all the pain and suffering for her to understand that no man walking on earth can give her the love GOD has ordained for her and her children. That is only possible through JESUS, everything we may not understand, but we must continue to look to the lord for our answers because only he knows our life from the beginning to the end. Sarah could have been dead a long time ago, but GOD had other plans.

She thought she was lost, but Sarah had to find her way through life trials and tribulation.Though she felt lost. Sarah never traveled those roads alone GOD was with her the whole time. GOD allowed Sarah to go through this journey because he knew she was going to come out stronger to help another one of his children. Sarah now lives with dignity and seek the lord and lead not to her own understanding an she is hopeful that one day she can form a stronger bond with her family. **If you or a loved one are having suicidal behavior or thoughts reach out to someone and call 1-800-273-8255(National Suicide Prevention Hotline).**

Made in the USA
Columbia, SC
30 March 2020